**Edited by Sally Smith**

September–December

**The Bible Reading Fellowship**
15 The Chambers, Vineyard
Abingdon OX14 3FE
brf.org.uk

The Bible Reading Fellowship (BRF) is a Registered Charity (233280)

ISBN 978 0 85746 455 2

Cover image © Edmund Cheng

**Acknowledgements**
Scripture quotations taken from The Holy Bible, New International Version (Anglicised edition) copyright © 1979, 1984, 2011 by Biblica. Used by permission of Hodder & Stoughton Publishers, a Hachette UK company. All rights reserved. 'NIV' is a registered trademark of Biblica. UK trademark number 1448790. • Scripture quotations from The New Revised Standard Version of the Bible, Anglicised edition, copyright © 1989, 1995 by the Division of Christian Education of the National Council of the Churches of Christ in the United States of America. Used by permission. All rights reserved. • Scripture quotations taken from the Holy Bible, New Living Translation, copyright © 1996, 2004, 2007, 2013. Used by permission of Tyndale House Publishers, Inc., Carol Stream, Illinois 60188. All rights reserved. • Scripture taken from THE MESSAGE. Copyright © 1993, 1994, 1995, 1996, 2000, 2001, 2002. Used by permission of NavPress Publishing Group. • Extracts from the Authorised Version of the Bible (The King James Bible), the rights in which are vested in the Crown, are reproduced by permission of the Crown's Patentee, Cambridge University Press. • Scripture taken from the New King James Version®. Copyright © 1982 by Thomas Nelson. Used by permission. All rights reserved. • Scripture quotations from the Good News Bible published by The Bible Societies/ HarperCollins Publishers Ltd, UK © American Bible Society 1966, 1971, 1976, 1992, used with permission. • Scripture quotations marked TPT are taken from The Psalms: Poetry on Fire, The Passion Translation®, copyright © 2014. Used by permission of BroadStreet Publishing Group, LLC, Racine, Wisconsin, USA. All rights reserved.

Extract from As a Child by Phil Steer, published by lulu.com, 2012.

pp. 102–103: 'Wachet auf' by Ann Lewin, used with kind permission.

Every effort has been made to trace and contact copyright owners for material used in this resource. We apologise for any inadvertent omissions or errors, and would ask those concerned to contact us so that full acknowledgement can be made in the future.

Printed by Gutenberg Press, Tarxien, Malta

# Sally Smith writes...

One of the things I love as editor of *Quiet Spaces* is not knowing what will be contained within an email from one of the writers. They each have their own style and preferences, but still each offering is an adventure waiting to happen, as well as reflecting the adventure already undertaken.

If it helps, see *Quiet Spaces* as a journey, an adventure. You may take the motorway and zoom from one end to the other in record time (speed limits permitting), or you may take the wandering tracks and lanes, taking the time to explore down some unmarked track and making some wonderful discoveries and meeting all sorts of people and creatures along the way.

In prayer, as in life, motorways and byways (and all the A and B roads in between) all have their place and their value. Motorways get us there quickly and generally with minimum stress, but are quite restrictive in where they go, and give no time to stop and linger and enjoy. Navigating main roads, you usually have some idea of where you are and they can get you to your destination reasonably quickly and with some flexibility. Lanes and tracks are essential when they lead to where you want to go, and are fun to explore, taking you to some unexpected places and giving a different perspective on the area, and they encourage you to wander and explore away from the planned route (if there ever was one).

So, as you travel through *Quiet Spaces*, notice what sort of road you are taking and check it is the right sort of road for you that day. Try to make some time to explore some of the tracks not on the plan; you never know where God will be waiting to meet you.

Happy travelling!

# Writers in this issue

**Janet Fletcher** is a priest in the Bro Ystumanner Ministry Area and the Bangor Diocesan Spirituality Officer. She facilitates and offers spiritual direction in the diocese, and enjoys teaching and writing about prayer and spirituality. She has written *Pathway to God* (SPCK, 2006) and has contributed to BRF's *Guidelines* Bible reading notes.

**Jean Marie Dwyer OP** is a Dominican nun of the Queen of Peace Monastery, Squamish, British Columbia, Canada. The monastery is dedicated to silence, prayer, study and intercession for all people. She is the author of *The Sacred Place of Prayer* (BRF, 2013) and *The Unfolding Journey: The God Within: Etty Hillesum and Meister Eckhart* (Novalis, 2014).

**Anne Noble** grew up on Merseyside and studied geology at Oxford and Toronto. She is an Associate Minister at Colton in the diocese of Lichfield and is married with two grown-up daughters. She still enjoys geology, reflecting on what we can hear and see of the God of all time through rocks. In her spare time, she loves gardening.

**Sally Welch** is Vicar of Charlbury and Area Dean of Chipping Norton. Sally also leads training events for the Diocese of Oxford in the area of spirituality and is a Diocesan Labyrinth Coordinator. She has written a number of books and is also the editor of BRF's *New Daylight* Bible reading notes.

**Helen Julian CSF** is an Anglican Franciscan sister and a priest, currently serving her community as Minister General. She has written three books for BRF and contributes to BRF's *New Daylight* Bible reading notes.

**Sue McCoulough** worked for a number of years at the BBC. She was then prayer Coordinator at Tearfund. Sue enjoys walking, creative writing and leading Quiet Days.

**Lynne Chitty** was a deacon at Gloucester Cathedral and now lives in a caravan in the grounds of Mill House Retreats in Devon. She combines leading creative writing courses with times of solitude and has a variety of rescue animals.

**Sally Smith** enjoys creating spaces that enable encounters with God through leading Quiet Days and creating prayer corners and stations. She has led prayer groups in her local church, works as a spiritual director and writes and produces educational materials.

**Dorinda Miller** has been leading Quiet Days and retreats in the UK and overseas, across denominations, for many years. As well as running Staying in the Vine, a six-week course on prayer and spiritual disciplines, she is currently developing audio meditation resources for www.into-deeper-waters.com.

# The woman at the well

*Janet Fletcher*

## The meeting

### Introduction

The story of the woman at the well is only found in John's Gospel (4:1–42). It is a long passage through which an unlikely and surprising conversation unfolds. It's a little like a question and answer session. In chapter 3 of John's Gospel, Jesus spoke with the Pharisee, Nicodemus, in the darkness of night; now, he speaks with a woman of Samaria in the brightness of the midday sun.

Samaria was a place, and a people, avoided by the Jews. Samaria had become an administrative centre in an area of Israel that had been taken over by the Assyrians in 722BC. The peoples had intermarried and worshipped a variety of gods, but when the Jews returned from exile in Babylon in 538BC, the Samaritans offered to help rebuild the Temple in Jerusalem. Their offer was turned down because they were not true 'Jews' any more. History, as we know, often has long fingers and a long memory in people's minds.

This story is one that crosses the boundaries of social and religious norms. This story, and ones like the Good Samaritan (Luke 10:25–37), would have shocked Jesus' listeners to the core. We find Jesus alone with a woman, whom he then engages in an ever-deepening conversation. No wonder the disciples were surprised when they returned.

Spend a little time reading through the story of the woman at the well. What strikes you about this story and all that takes place within these verses? What questions would you like to ask?

# Into the depths

## Reflective

John's Gospel is full of symbolism and contrast, imagery and texture. In this reading, we can imagine the heat and the light coming from the sun, and the coolness of the water deep down in the darkness of the well. Stones were placed with care to form the well, and they give to it strength and purpose. The well provides water for the cattle and sheep as well as for the community of Samaritans. In contrast is the assumed 'weakness' of the woman who comes at such a strange time of day to draw up water.

We find that, although the woman is vulnerable in coming to an isolated place, she has both inner strength and insight into her own self: the rough and the smooth. She deliberately comes to the well at a time when she knows she is unlikely to meet anyone else. On this day, though, she encounters a stranger who will transform her life.

She is not ignored, or despised, but welcomed as Jesus asks her for a drink. Through the conversation which then takes place, she opens up her life to the stranger who seems to know all about her. She acknowledges the truth about her relationship with the man she lives with, and also shares her belief that the promised Messiah will come.

Jesus listens, and so enables the woman to talk about what is important to her. Through his listening, the woman is able to search deep within her own self, to the truth of her life and to the faith which dwells within her.

To be listened to is a great gift, especially when that listening is not judgemental or seeking to give a solution to a problem, but simply to be alongside another person. This is a listening that is offered with unconditional love. How easy is it to be so truthful to another person as the woman was with Jesus? How much do we keep to ourselves, and why?

Who truly listens to you in quietness and love?

Who listens to you explore your own life of faith?

Who do you listen to? Who can you find time to listen to this week?

# At the well

## Imaginative

Find a time and a place where you can sit comfortably in prayer without being disturbed.

As you sit, close your eyes and become aware of any sounds around you.

Acknowledge them and let them rest where they are.

Ask God to be with you as you journey within, seeking his peace and love.

Slowly, imagine you are travelling through the layers of your inner self until you reach a pool of tranquil water at the core of your being.

Rest awhile at this pool, the well of your being. What does the water look like? Is it clear, warm or cool? Do you dip your fingers or toes into the water, or do you drink from it?

In this place, there is safety and love.

In this place, you can be vulnerable.

In this place, you are embraced by God's love.

In this place, you are cherished for the person you are and the person you can yet become.

Imagine seeing Jesus walk across to you. Invite him to sit and drink.

What is the conversation that then takes place?

What will you tell him?

When you are ready, leave this pool of tranquil water, the well of your being.

Slowly, make your prayerful journey back to the present moment.

Afterwards, it would be helpful to make a note in a journal of the experience of your thoughts and feelings during this prayer. It may be that you feel the need to talk to someone, maybe your minister, spiritual director or close friend.

# The water of life

### Reflective

Before water reaches the well, it has already undertaken a long journey. The rain falls upon the earth and, touching the mountain top, it weaves its way downwards and inwards. The rain nourishes and feeds the earth and enables the growth of creation's seeds. Water trickles a path into streams and rivers before greeting the ocean.

Somewhere along its way, some water will find its natural course diverted. It is collected within a given space, an appropriate place where it can give life to a gathered community. Early groups of people would settle near a well or a place of running water, knowing their dependence upon it. The gathered water would not be stagnant or undrinkable, but moving, flowing and life-giving.

The paradox of water is that, while it can cause devastation and take life, it is also necessary for our everyday living. We cannot do without water.

Talking to children about water within the context of baptism, I ask first what they think we need water for. It often brings a mixed array of answers! Water to keep us healthy and to make our plants grow—even water to keep us clean often comes with a little prompting. We will look at the water of baptism later.

Jesus offers the woman at the well the water of life, saying that those who take this water will be as 'a spring of water gushing up to eternal life' (John 4:14 NRSV). Here, Jesus moves the imagery away from actual physical water to the water which leads to faith in God and the flowing movement of the Holy Spirit within the depths of our being.

Our journey of faith is long and ongoing. At times, like the water finding its way down a mountainside, we will stumble over rocks and rubble as well as soft grass. We will come to the well, where we will find a deepening relationship with God. Like the water in the well, our life generally and in faith will continue to move, to be refreshed and challenged. The water of life reminds us not to let our lives or our faith become static and stagnant, but to keep them alive and active.

How alive or stagnant do you feel your life of faith is at the moment?

Can you find some water or an image of water that reflects this? Spend time there telling God about it and listening to his viewpoint.

# Water

### Poetry

*Sky and earth combine in an essence of life-giving power, flowing
as water urges the ground to move away,
creating its own footprint on mountain ravine, stream, and
out of the extremes of heat and sand
an oasis in dry arid ground, life for creation.*

*Water of life, essential, gathered together, cleaned,
piped into fortunate homes, water on tap, easily acquired,
without thinking or acknowledgement
of the sky above or the ground below, the people involved
in the bringing of the daily water into our homes.*

*Water clear and fresh, water dirty and muddy, yet drunk*
*out of need, to keep alive. We, who drink of it, clear from tap*
*or plastic bottle, do we consider those who*
*do not have our luxury? Do we consider those who*
*seek their life-giving water from the depths of a well?*

*Sky and earth combine in an essence of life-giving power, power*
*for destruction as well as for health and growth within us and*
   *around us.*
*Water to be conserved, shared out. Water to be valued not wasted*
*in our homes. Water to refresh our inner as well as our outer being,*
*strengthening our own life within creation.*

Take time to think about the amount of water you use each day and
whether you could use less.

 Is there a charity you could support that brings clean water to
those most in need across the world?

# Being creative

### Going out

Children seem to enjoy jumping into puddles; as adults, though, we
are more likely to step over them! I am very fortunate in living on the
coast. The sea, which I can see from my upstairs study window, is
only a ten-minute walk away. I have to admit that most of my walks
to the beach and the sea usually take place when I have visitors.

 If you live close enough to the sea, take the time to walk along
the beach. Look out to the horizon. What does the sea look like? Is
it calm, or are there lots of waves? Look at the sand and all that the
sea brings to shore—the pebbles, the shells and the rock pools. On
this walk, you may wish to simply sit, look out and ponder. What
comes to mind?

On this walk, remember the story from John's Gospel. If there is a rock or place to sit, take a rest and quietly think about a conversation you would have with Jesus in this place. You may like to draw the scene you see, or write down the words and phrases that come to you at this time. If you can, dig into the sand as though making a well. The sand will become wet through the underlying water from the sea, or will fill with water as the tide comes in.

Prayerfully sit with God and all you feel he is calling you to; how he is seeking to fill your life with the water of life. Become aware of what you may need to give up or let go of. Imagine placing those things into the well you have made. As they are washed away, they have not disappeared but become a part of the greater whole—of the sea and of yourself. They will be a part of the shaping of all that is to come.

If you cannot make a journey to the beach and sea, you may have some other water you could visit and adapt the exercise, or you could imagine it in your own mind. Imagine that you are there to experience the sounds of the waves and the salty smell of the sea. You may wish to fill a washing-up bowl with water to put your feet in or, even, sit in the bath. Instead of digging a well, you may want to draw a picture of a well on paper, and then write in it your thoughts.

# The water of faith

## Reflective

The woman came to the well at midday so she wouldn't meet anyone. She came to draw up water to drink: water to keep her body healthy and functioning. She came to the well that was known through history as the well given by their ancestor Jacob. She knows the story, and she also knows about the promised Messiah, coming to proclaim God's word.

She is a woman of spiritual longing, seeking the water of life itself. She seeks the water Jesus offers to her. Her journey towards a deepening faith has already begun.

No matter what our theology or understanding of baptism is, integral to baptism is water. Even today, many still seek out the Church for baptism. They may come with little understanding of what baptism and the Christian faith means to them, and their ongoing life.

What does baptism mean to you? What, if anything, do you remember about your own baptism?

Baptism is only the beginning, for a journey in faith after baptism is one that each person needs to decide upon for themselves. God is present, but waits, as Jesus did with the woman, for a conversation that will begin the transformation from unbelief into faith.

In this new awareness of her own being and the gift of the water of life, the woman returns to her village. She does not hide away, but openly proclaims that she has met a man who knows all about her, and who told her he is the promised Messiah. Her words lead others to Jesus.

Baptism draws us through the water into the family of God's Church. Like the woman at the well, we too are to proclaim the good news of Jesus. How do you proclaim the good news?

Maybe ask your minister if you can go along to a baptism preparation class or to be present at a baptism, especially if baptism doesn't take place within your usual service, or if it is a while since you last attended a baptism service. What thoughts and feelings come to mind? Hold on to those who are to be baptised in prayer to God, asking that they may come to follow the way of Jesus in their lives.

You may like to anoint yourself with the baptism water after the service by marking your hands or forehead with a cross.

# I return to the well

## Story

*It's a beautiful day. The sun is still shining, and there is a gentle breeze giving relief from the heat of the day as the evening approaches. I no longer come to the well at midday. My whole life has changed. It changed the day I met a stranger at the well.*

*He is the promised Messiah. Somehow I knew that was who he was. I could feel the love that flowed from him. Not a love I was afraid of, but gentle, welcoming and challenging. It was a love that looked deep into me and knew me, even though we had never met before that day.*

*We talked. That conversation should never have taken place—I'm a woman and a Samaritan—but I'm so glad it did. He didn't bother about social conventions! On that day I became someone new even though everything remained the same. The difference was in me. That difference meant that I simply ran back and shouted that I had met the Messiah. No wonder people stared at me. I hardly spoke to anyone before, and always hid away.*

*All that has changed. I am still me, but more so, if that makes sense. I take part in village life in a way I hadn't done for a very long time. I feel accepted.*

*I'm learning what it means to worship God in spirit and truth. I come to the well, to sit quietly and pray. I still draw the water to drink for my bodily and physical well-being. In my heart I know that, through that meeting, God's Spirit is within me—the water he spoke of, the water of eternal life. Maybe one day, all people can come together to worship God, on the mountainside and in the Temple.*

Do you have ecumenical services where different traditions and denominations come together to worship God? What does it feel like to be a part of that gathering?

# Prayer of blessing

## Prayer

For this time of prayer, have in front of you a bowl with water in it, and maybe a floating candle.

> *Within all of creation, O God,*
> *bless water to dry and arid places,*
> *bless water to the earth for nourishment and growth,*
> *bless water to the thirsty, clear and safe to drink.*
>
> *Within all creation, O God,*
> *bless the water of our streams, rivers and oceans,*
> *bless the water of many colours, calm and dangerous,*
> *bless the water for the life force it gives to those dwelling within.*
>
> *Within all creation, O God,*
> *bless the skills of those who gather water,*
> *bless the engineering plants and facilities which clean water,*
> *bless those who feed to our taps our daily water.*
>
> *Within all creation, O God,*
> *bless the water which draws us to prayer,*
> *bless the water through which we were baptised,*
> *bless the water, symbol of eternal life.*
> *Amen*

What other areas of blessing would you include?
Write your own prayer on the theme of water.

# The water of renewal

## Meditative

Find a quiet time and space to sit and be with God. If it's possible, and comfortable to you, then this may be prayer outdoors near the sea or a stream, or simply in the garden.

You may wish to use again a bowl filled with water and place in it a floating candle. Have with you a glass of water to drink from.

Begin by getting comfortable, and take a few deep breaths in and out.

Listen to the sounds around you—what are those sounds and where are they coming from?

These sounds are a part of creation; listen to them, and let them go.

Look with your eyes, or with your imagination, at the water in front of you—its colour, its movement, maybe its scent. This water is safe. This water will not harm you.

Wherever this water touches, it will not bring destruction, but growth and new beginning.

This water will nourish the earth. It will nourish you. Take a drink of water from your glass. Feel the water in your mouth—water seeking to bring to you a sense and feeling of renewal.

Sit quietly for a while with your own body's need for renewal and healing—what is needed?

When you are ready, take another drink of water. Feel the water cleansing your mouth.

Sit quietly for a while with your own need for cleansing, for forgiving—what is needed?

When you are ready, take another drink of water. Feel the water in your mouth bringing you refreshment.

Sit quietly for a while with your own need for refreshment and renewal in your life journey and in your faith journey.

What is your prayer at this moment? Ask God for the renewal in life you seek.

When you are ready, end this time of quietness by giving thanks to God, and make a note of anything you feel is important to be remembered.

# Intricate weaving

## Reflective

The intricate weaving of stone upon stone provides the necessary strength to support the structure of the well. It provides a separation between the earth that is on one side and the water it holds within it. The framework of the well needs careful thought. It needs to be carefully constructed and built. Within this framework of human construction is the memory of touch, of stories told, of those who gathered at the well for water to drink.

The writer of Psalm 139 saw the intricate weaving of our bodies, declaring to God that, 'it was you who formed my inward parts; you knit me together in my mother's womb' (v. 13). The psalmist continues, saying, 'My frame was not hidden from you, when I was being made in secret, intricately woven in the depths of the earth' (v. 15).

Our outer framework holds within it all that is necessary for life, for the working of each bone, sinew and organ. Yet, like the structure of the well, there is also so much that we cannot see with the eye, but need to feel in our heart. In our heart, and in our mind, is our memory. In our memory is all that has touched us throughout our lives to this point in time, and will continue to do so. Our memory holds within it our experiences of life, our relationships, our personal and our shared stories.

We cannot usually see the very bottom of a well, but we know that it has still been touched by life and the elements of the weather. We, too, are 'weathered' by our lives, and the joys and struggles we face. Regardless of the shape of our lives, our outer framework, we are intricately and wonderfully woven, and our strength comes from our relationship with God, and those we love. We each have a gift to offer to others. We each have a part to play in the weaving of life-giving water—of love and peace—in this world.

What is your most precious memory? As you relive it, notice where God is present. Receive the memory afresh as a gift from him.

# Looking into the well

## Reflective

Living in Wales, there are many wells associated with various saints nearby. Each has its own story of how it came into being, how it became a place of healing and pilgrimage. Are there any wells near to you, close enough to visit? These wells are a part of our story and heritage.

Read again the story of the woman at the well in John's Gospel, 4:1–42.

What thoughts and questions come to mind?

For the woman, the well was a place of necessity: it was the place from which to draw water. It became a place of healing too. Through the encounter with Jesus, a transformation took place which changed the woman. It brought to her new life and new energy. It brought to her a sense of welcome and acceptance, and restored to her a place in society. Those from the village listened to her words and with her went to see Jesus. The villagers' conversations with the woman continue as they tell her they believe not only because of her story, but because they have seen and heard it for themselves. She isn't ignored, but drawn into the community.

How does the story of the woman speak into your own life, the life of the church and life in the wider world?

Through this story, what may God be now asking of you?

*O God, refresh me with the water of life,*
*may I see the beauty of your presence in the people I meet,*
*may I be aware of the intricate weaving of all our stories,*
*may my story be one of love and peace and renewal.*
*Amen*

# The fruit of kindness

*Jean Marie Dwyer OP*

## Kindness

### Introduction

Kindness is often viewed as mere courtesy or as an insignificant Christian practice, but the Bible emphasises kindness and considers it a major Christian virtue: a fruit of the Holy Spirit.

Kindness is a disposition we develop by serving our brothers and sisters in love through kindly deeds. This humble way of serving is a powerful means for transforming our lives, and a way of gifting our neighbour.

In the following sections, we will explore some of the biblical words related to kindness and their interconnectedness as part of the Spirit-filled fruitfulness of our Christian life. There will be a biblical study section on what it means to be fruitful disciples.

The various sections all lead to growth in our understanding of how the fruit of kindness can transform our lives and the lives of our brothers and sisters by our practical deeds.

Pause and consider any acts of kindness you have committed in the last 24 hours, and any that you have witnessed or experienced from others. Hold before God the kind people you know.

Slowly eat a piece of fruit. As you do so, be reminded of the abundant gifts of fruit and their juiciness and sweetness, the way they give completely and unconditionally, often overflowing with juice. Remember this image of fruit as you explore the fruit of kindness.

# Biblical kindness

## Spotlight

The fruit of the Spirit listed in Galatians is:

> *… love, joy, peace, patience, kindness, generosity, faithfulness, gentleness, and self-control. There is no law against such things… If we live by the Spirit, let us also be guided by the Spirit.*
>
> 5:22–23, 25 NRSV

These nine characteristics form the spiritual physiognomy of a Spirit-filled disciple of Jesus. Galatians 5:22–23 defines what our life looks like when we live in the Spirit. The text from Galatians is not enumerating a list of virtues but is describing a follower of Jesus producing fruit for the kingdom of God. What a beautiful description! This text teaches us that our life will produce fruit when we surrender totally to the Holy Spirit as our formatter and guide. We surrender by being patient, kind, generous, peaceful, full of love, faithful, peaceable, gentle and self-controlled. All these characteristics become ours by our daily choices and through God's grace.

The Greek word (*chrestotes*) translated as kindness refers to 'divine kindness': God's loving-kindness toward us. Our acts of kindness are meant to reflect God's loving-kindness. Kindness in this sense produces a goodness that is practical, and meets the needs of our neighbour with tender-hearted love and respect.

Biblical kindness, as a fruit of the Spirit, is also connected to gestures of compassion to those in need. The fruit of kindness enables us to be sensitive and gentle in perceiving the needs of our neighbour in God's way, with love, gentleness and compassion.

To understand some of the extended meanings in the Greek, do a Google search: 'Greek text analysis of Galatians 5:22'. You can see the English and the Greek and the various meanings at www.biblehub.com.

# Christian fruitfulness

## Bible study

A fruit is something that is produced from its source; so, apples come from apple trees and strawberries from strawberry plants. Likewise, loving actions and concern for our neighbour come from our life of Spirit-filled discipleship.

When we live in the Spirit, our actions towards our neighbour produce the fruit of holiness in us, and convey God's loving presence to others. Our Christian life becomes fruitful in the works of the kingdom. When we allow the Spirit to become manifest in the way we live our life, we testify to the transforming work of the Holy Spirit at work within us. Our fruitfulness is God's gift. Kindness, as a fruit of the Holy Spirit, helps us to reflect the mystery of God's loving-kindness and steadfast love to every human being through our human action. Kindness involves love, longsuffering, and goodness leading to joy, peace and self-control.

It is impossible to produce genuine Christ-like kindness as described in Galatians 5:22 by ourselves. A new heart is required. The fruit of kindness forms our inner heart and pours over into kindness towards all we meet. Then a growth process follows, which can only take place as we submit to, and obey, the Holy Spirit.

The fruit of the Spirit within us can be compared to a healthy vine or a tree which brings forth the best and sweetest fruit of virtue and holiness. This is the image used in the following biblical passages to describe the fruitfulness of discipleship.

Take one of the sections below and write as you reflect on the unified message of the texts, including your conclusions or the lessons you have learned. Then end with a short prayer.

**1. By his death and resurrection Christ becomes the first fruits of those to be saved—Christ first and then all who belong to Christ.**

- 1 Corinthians 15:20–23
- James 1:18
- Romans 8:23
- Romans 11:16
- Revelation 14:4–5

**2. Good and bad fruit: We are known by our fruit.**

- Matthew 3:8–10
- Matthew 7:16–20
- Luke 6:43–44
- James 3:17
- Revelation 14:4–5

**3. Jesus is the true vine.**

- John 15:1–17

The image of Jesus as the true vine is a powerful image of our relationship to one another in Christ, our head.

God has first chosen us, to live our life in love for God and for our neighbour. There are no strangers because God has called us his friends and appointed us to bear fruit that will last. We produce fruit by leading others into the friendship of Christ.

What are the consequences of discipleship? What is required in order to remain living branches of the vine?

How does the text you have read explain the power of Scripture in our lives?

Who is the absolute source of our fruitfulness? Do we fully live our life from that source? What do we need to change?

# God's loving-kindness toward us

## Creative

The biblical term 'loving-kindness' refers to acts of kindness motivated by love. It is used primarily as an attribute of God. The Old and New Testaments depict God's kindness as universal, extended to the good and the wicked. God's kindness is meant to lead to repentance. The divine loving-kindness is fully manifested in the salvation brought to us in Christ Jesus. Our salvation derives from God's loving-kindness and continued presence to us in love and mercy.

Paul, in his letter to Titus, teaches that God chose us not because we were righteous but because of his great mercy. In the humanity of Jesus, God brought to us his mercy and a 'rebirth and renewal by the Holy Spirit' (Titus 3:5). In Romans, Paul tells us that God proves his love for us in that Jesus died for us while we were yet sinners (Romans 5:7–8).

God's loving-kindness is our model for our kindness to others. Reflect on the qualities of God's loving-kindness. They are:

- Totally self-giving without depending on our worthiness
- Compassionate and merciful
- Always there for us
- Transforming us

Make a list of how the attributes of God's loving-kindness can be translated into ways of practising kindness to others. It is little acts of kindness that help us to grow in love and delicate attentiveness to others. Seek to be attentive to the needs of those around you. Acts of kindness are directed to the real needs of the other.

In what particular ways can you show kindness:

- Towards various members of your family?
- In your workplace?
- With your friends?
- With strangers you meet?

Use this list to map out your daily practice of kindness.

# Responding to God's loving-kindness

## Reflective

God's love for us does not depend on our goodness but on God's grace and mercy. We love God because he first loved us. Even our response to God is initiated by the Holy Spirit's movement within us. In the first letter of John we learn that, because God has loved us, we should love one another, and by doing this we are perfected (1 John 4:7–12).

As a young girl I was very shy. When I began high school I took the city bus to school. Several girls from my freshman class got on the bus a few stops before me. They were always talking and laughing and seemed so nice. But I was too shy to approach them. One of the girls noticed me and drew me into the group. Her sensitive kindness was the beginning of a bond of friendship that lasted through high school and continues even now in our adult years.

What Karon did in drawing me into the group was an act of kindness, flowing from goodness and compassion to an outsider. She was sensitively attentive to me as a person and saw a need to which she responded.

- How might your relationships with others change if you responded with kindness?
- How often do you fail to recognise the outsider as a sister or brother, who is longing to be included?
- Does the kindness you show to others reflect God's kindness to us?

# Reflecting God

## Reflective

Our loving-kindness finds its pattern in God's loving-kindness. Being kind to others seems like such a small gesture. But a kindly spirit transforms our whole life. When we show the loving-kindness of God through our service to our neighbour, we display sentiments of tenderness and usefulness to others. The Spirit-filled source of our kindness will radiate outwardly to those we seek to serve. The indwelling Spirit produces the fruit that will transform us and impart to us the power to call our brothers and sisters into a godly way of life.

Because of our brokenness, our imitation of God's kindness does not come naturally, but acting kindly can become a consistent component of our Christian living. Through openness to the Holy Spirit, the divine kindness is reflected in our human experience of loving and giving. What we have been given freely by God is to be distributed freely by us through our loving deeds of kindness. We are truly children of God when we exhibit God's kindness and mercy. We are asked to be lovingly kind and compassionate to our brothers and sisters, like Jesus. Paul, in his letter to the Romans, maps out what this means:

*Indeed, rarely will anyone die for a righteous person—though perhaps for a good person someone might actually dare to die. But God proves his love for us in that while we still were sinners Christ died for us.*

ROMANS 5:7–8

In this text, Paul tells us it is rare for anyone to die for a good person, yet Jesus died for us while we yet were sinners. If our model is Jesus then we are called to be willing to not only die, but live for sinners—for the poor, for the unlovely, the outcast and those who are shunned. What does this mean? In our culture it is the successful, beautiful, dynamic, rich and popular ones who are sought out. Often the reason that we are attracted to these people is for what they can do for us, the ways that they can promote our well-being.

The path of kindly living is so much more radical. Our kindness must be universal, frequently expressed in small and often hidden ways without seeking a return.

Luke's Gospel echoes the same teaching we found in Romans:

*If you lend to those from whom you hope to receive, what credit is that to you? Even sinners lend to sinners, to receive as much again. But love your enemies, do good, and lend, expecting nothing in return. Your reward will be great, and you will be children of the Most High; for he is kind to the ungrateful and the wicked. Be merciful, just as your Father is merciful.*

LUKE 6:34–36

Read the text from Luke slowly and prayerfully.

Each sentence leads us deeper into Jesus' teaching.

Pick out the key words for you and spend some time with them.

Write down in your journal the ways this text calls you to extend God's kindness to others. In what ways do you find that your acts of kindness are impacted by the other characteristics of a Spirit-filled life as listed in Galatians 5:22?

Write a reflection on what you have discovered, and how this new knowledge impacts in practical ways on your Christian life.

# Recognising the dignity of the other

## Going out

How often do we just walk by people without noticing them? Do we really see the people we work with every day? We need to live our life mindfully attentive to the people we encounter during our day. Sadly, rudeness and insensitivity seem to be a way of life for many in our modern culture. The uniqueness of each person is often lost in our anonymous society. Everyone is precious and cherished in God's sight. Our call as disciples of Jesus is to unequivocally show sensitivity and kindness towards everyone we meet, even strangers. Each person is a child of God, even the crankiest.

We need courage and the willingness to make room for kindness in our daily schedules. Being a kind person is a gift of our self to others. It may mean changing routines, taking more time for other people and developing a new attitude that is best expressed by the spiritual attitude described in Philippians 2:3–4 (NKJV):

> *Let nothing be done through selfish ambition or conceit, but in lowliness of mind let each esteem others better than himself. Let each of you look out not only for his own interests, but also for the interests of others.*

How can we show kindness, consideration and respect for others?

Our example of kindness reshapes our hearts and touches the hearts of others.

As parents, we can teach our children to be sensitive and kind to the girl or boy who feels excluded, or is not popular, and draw them into the circle of their friendship.

We can give a gift of a kind and happy smile to people we pass in the street, or meet in the store or other public forums. Our gift is in the smile, not in what we receive in return. We just keep smiling with love. Kindness is catching.

Next time you walk into a room, look around and notice who is there. Look at each person with new eyes. As you pass people today, really look at them, and say a kind word or give a cheerful greeting. In the Spirit we are called to make every person feel special and of worth. Kindness is an ongoing commitment to live the gospel.

# Kindness and loving service

## Reflective

The Greek word which translates as 'kindness' (*chrestotes*) means that kindness is an act towards our neighbour that is useful. Our kindness to our brother or sister is an act of helpful service done in love. Gradually we develop a habit of kindness to others. It won't happen overnight, but the more you show kindness, the more your daily life will be transformed. Practise kindness without any thought of reward. This is the real challenge. Often we think in terms of what is fair, but God gives to each of us as we need and not necessarily in equal measure. This is the example we are called to follow.

Don't waste opportunities for kindness. They often come around several times a day.

If you miss an opportunity, then show kindness the next time that situation arises.

Each time we reach out in kindness, it is a learning process that impacts on who we are and how we see the other.

Be attentive to the needs of those around you. Draw people out, make them feel welcome, important and valued. What a gift this is to another!

How can you really see the other as precious, unique and of infinite value?

Do you engage with others? Are you sensitive to others? List some ways you can develop these qualities. Draw on the ways God has developed these in you.

# Kindness and forgiveness

## Prayer

One of the hardest teachings of Jesus to put into practice is 'love your enemies' (Luke 6:35). We sometimes have trouble loving our friends when they irritate us because of one thing or another. How can we be kind and tender-hearted to those who do us wrong, or do not like us, or who seem always to be hurtful to others? To do so is really a challenge.

Following this precept is the test of our faithful discipleship. Opening our hearts to the movement of the Holy Spirit enables us to live out the Gospel dictates of selfless giving in loving-kindness and forgiveness. The Gospel of Luke asks us to do good to the grateful and ungrateful, the good and the evil, friend and enemy. What credit do we have if we are kind only to those who are kind to us (Luke 6:27–36)? Only when we extend kindness and forgiveness to EVERYONE can we be called children of God. Kindness teaches us to look deeper with the eyes of mercy. Wow—tall order!

Write a prayer of forgiveness for someone who has offended you. In the prayer, ask God to forgive you for your sins and lack of kindness and mercy to others. Include in your prayer some specific occasions when you have failed to be kind, especially to someone who is hard to love or has offended you. Ask God the Father to forgive and heal them as he has forgiven and healed you. Ask also for strength to become a loving and kind person and for God to show you practical ways you can do this. Pray for the grace of the Holy Spirit to live a spirit-filled life. End the prayer with words of gratitude and praise.

# Be tender-hearted

### Meditative

Paul, in his letter to the Ephesians, exhorts us to be kind and tender-hearted to one another (Ephesians 4:32). The word tender-hearted is translated from a Greek word which carries the connotation of a deep gut-wrenching compassion. In Colossians, Paul says God has chosen us to be holy so we must clothe ourselves 'with tender-hearted mercy, kindness, humility, gentleness and patience' (Colossians 3:12 NLT). In silent prayer, reflect on the word 'tender-hearted' and its relation to the other words in the Colossians passage. The word 'tenderness' evokes in us certain emotions and ways of responding.

Visualise an experience when you felt tenderness for someone. Take time to relive that encounter in your imagination. How did you express it? Rest in the feelings of that moment.

Or: Visualise an experience of having received tenderness from a friend or family member. Picture the encounter in your imagination. Reflect on what it meant for you at the time.

- What were your feelings? How did it change you?
- Was it a moment of peace and serenity?
- How can you take that gift of tenderness and share it with others?

# The transformative power of kindness

## Imaginative

Sit in a quiet place.

Imagine what a world full of kindness would be like. Rest in that thought. It might help to write a description of what it would be like.

Bring to mind someone you know who is kind. Hold them before God. How do they manifest kindness? What effect do they have on others? How has their kindness affected you?

Imagine yourself as a kind person. What would you be like? Write a description. What do you have to do to be that person?

*O God, give me a kind heart. Let the fruit of your Spirit—love, joy, peace, patience, kindness, generosity, faithfulness, gentleness, and self-control—fill my heart and spill over into my daily choices and ways of serving my brothers and sisters. Help me to see everyone I meet with your vision. Each person is so precious to you. Let each person find an equal place in my heart as a brother or sister. The beauty of each person is so much deeper than what I first perceive. Give me a tender-hearted and compassionate kindness, a gentle spirit to receive my neighbour with love, and to serve them in the way that is needful. Give me courage and steadfastness to walk in the way of kindness. Let me be kindly in all my dealings and in every chance that comes my way so that I may become a kind person. Forgive me when I fail and help me to begin again. My Lord, I know that the gift of kindness has the power to transform my heart, and everything around me.*
*Amen*

# Kindness

## Reflective

Kindness is such a gentle and humble word, but it has the strength and power to heal and transform us. Jesus was a kind person. He said of himself, 'Learn from me; for I am... humble in heart' (Matthew 11:29 NRSV). Kindness thrives on humble deeds. Jesus touched those he met with such tenderness and compassion. He really saw and was present to each person. Tenderness, compassion, mercy and humility are characteristics of a kind person.

The fruit of kindness helps us to meet the needs of our brothers and sisters with a gentle attentiveness that is without harshness. To put our self aside for the sake of a sister or brother. To be kind just in order to be kind. The practice of kindness is linked with the joy of the Spirit. When we are truly kind, we find great joy in serving our brothers and sisters—a joy that is not of this world. It is a manifestation of God's kingdom in our midst.

Our kindness towards our sisters and brothers should be pure gift, reflecting God's abundant gift of love to us. Kindness flows from our life in the Spirit and, like God, we extend our loving-kindness to all we meet. Our kindness becomes a participation in God's loving-kindness and reflects God's tender mercy to all we meet. May we live a kindly life through inexhaustible resources of the gentle, yet dynamic, Holy Spirit poured into our hearts.

*Lord, help me to extend your kindness to everyone. Not only to those I love or find attractive, but to those who are opponents and unattractive. Give me a universal kindness, a reflection of your divine kindness that you pour out on me each day.*
*Amen*

This is what the fruit of kindness is all about. Its fruitfulness comes from the indwelling Spirit who guides us and transforms us.

Kindness is a humble virtue with great power for good.

As Spirit-filled Christians we have been given the power to transform the world by our works of loving-kindness.

# Jacob

*Anne Noble*

## Jacob's struggle

### Introduction

Jacob's story in the book of Genesis begins before he is born in the hopes and prayers of his father Isaac for his wife Rebekah (Genesis 25:21). After pre-birth struggles with his twin Esau, themes of trickery, deception and favouritism pervade the story in which Esau (the elder son) is steadily deprived of birthright and blessing. Throughout Jacob's life, there are journeys and periods of waiting and serving. He amasses wealth, experiences loss, worries and struggles and at times God can seem very far from the heart of the text. Yet at key moments, Jacob encounters God in ways which change his life and direction.

Jacob's is an epic story spanning nearly 25 chapters of the book of Genesis. We cannot follow it all here, so we will focus on the story as it is told in Genesis chapter 25:19 through to 33:11. Stop and read the passages now and, as you do so, what themes seem important to you? Where do you notice God in the story? What are your initial reactions to Jacob, both likes and dislikes?

Write your thoughts down and keep them to hand as we enter Jacob's story in more detail.

*Ever-present God, help us to hear you in Jacob's story and to recognise your presence in our own.*
*Amen*

# The struggle in Rebekah

## Reflective

In our next two reflections, we will look at the beginning of Jacob's story. Commence by reading Genesis 25:19–34.

Jacob and his twin brother Esau are answers to prayer. Their mother Rebekah had been barren for 20 years when Isaac prays to God for her, and God responds with the longed-for pregnancy. However, what should have been a time of joyful expectation becomes a nightmare. In those days, pregnancy was surrounded with uncertainty and danger. It is doubtful that Rebekah would have known that she was carrying twins, yet she is aware that something is wrong, sensing the struggle within her. The word used in the Hebrew to describe this struggle is a strong one. It evokes feelings of almost crushing oppression, of breaking and smashing as the two babies jostle in the womb. No wonder Rebekah is driven to both physical and spiritual despair as she recognises the ominous nature of the symptoms. Perhaps she feared both for her life and reason as well as the safety of her unborn children as she cries out, 'If it is to be this way, why do I live?' (v. 22). Her prayers for a child have been answered, yet now Rebekah doesn't understand—what should have brought happiness is actually the cause of pain.

God's rather ambiguous answer to her does nothing to end the anguish but will bring understanding to it—even though God's words are a warning that her distress is a sign of things to come.

Whether we can enter the precise nature of Rebekah's distress at this point or not, many of us will have experienced the spiritual, mental and sometimes even physical pain when something we have hoped for doesn't turn out as we expected. These are occasions when we may question God and wonder, 'Why me?'

This part of the story asks questions of faith. What happens when prayers seem answered but the answer is not straightforward, is unclear or even challenges belief? How do we deal with disappointment, our own and other people's?

Offer your own experiences of struggle and disappointment to God. If it helps, you could write your own prayer of protest seeking understanding for times when your hopes and prayers have not been answered as you wished.

# Reflecting on Rebekah's pain

### Creative/Reflective

In Rebekah's case, the cause of her suffering and God's response to it only become clear when she gives birth—she has been carrying twins. Rebekah's story introduces themes of struggle and difficult answers to prayer to the text. For many, living with these twin themes is a daily reality. Offer your own experiences of these to God.

Read 2 Corinthians 12:7–10.

God does not inflict pain and suffering on us, but these are a part of human experience that God is only too aware of, both through his love and care and through the suffering of Jesus in Gethsemane and on the cross. In the passage from 2 Corinthians, Paul struggles with an unidentified 'thorn in the flesh'. For reasons beyond Paul's understanding, God does not remove the pain but does give Paul the strength to live with it.

Find a thorn (be careful) and mount it carefully on a piece of card. Write out God's response to Paul beside it (2 Corinthians 12:9). Reflect on its purpose in the right place—what it brings to a plant, how the thorn might seem from the plant's point of view.

Now reflect on how it seems to us as a source of pain and irritation, both physical and mental. Contemplate the ambiguity of how something which protects in the right place can be a cause of harm in another.

Offer your thoughts and reflections to God.

# Birthright

**Reflective**

Read Genesis 25:27–34. Esau is the elder of the twins by a matter of minutes, yet even in the story of his birth there is the sense that Jacob is nipping at his heels. As the oldest son, Esau will become head of the family on Isaac's death, as well as receiving a larger share of the inheritance. In this story, Esau sells this privilege and right to Jacob for bread and stew. You might wonder whether Esau, a skilled hunter, was really in such a bad place and so hungry that this transaction was absolutely necessary, or whether his senses and perhaps even greed took over in that moment and led him to give away something truly precious in exchange for fleeting satisfaction.

Take a few moments to wonder what is really precious to you. Would you really give this away so easily?

*Father God, you gave your one and only Son, the most precious part of you, to be life for us. Help us to appreciate your love in both the gift and the giving, and to reflect that in our lives.*
*Amen*

# Blessing

**Intercession**

Genesis 26:34—28:9 forms a pivotal part of the story of Jacob and explains why he left his home and began his travels, during which he will encounter God and come to a new understanding of his calling. Reread this part of the story and, as you do so, note particularly how the narrator engages all our senses and describes some very raw emotions. What strikes you? Where and with whom do your sympathies lie, if anywhere or with anyone?

Notice how the characters leave God out of their plans—God neither speaks, nor is consulted. Yet, the blessing that Isaac wishes to pass on to his son Esau, but confers instead on Jacob, calls on God's gracious and bountiful presence. You might wish to take a moment to live with the paradox of that.

Many of us experience life in this way: periods when God feels as close as breathing, in which we listen for and hear God's voice and experience his call, and then times when that closeness seems to have gone, God seems silent or we choose not to approach God.

This particularly sad episode in the story indicates how broken the family has become. Divided by Esau's marriages to foreign women, the favouritism of the parents (Isaac for Esau and Rebekah for Jacob) and suspicion of one another (listening at doors, seeking spies within the camp), the family is living a life of complicity, deceit and scheming which inevitably brings brokenness and pain. Now Jacob has to leave home, Isaac is a broken man, Esau has murderous thoughts in his heart and Rebekah will drop out of the narrative until it is mentioned that she has died (Genesis 49:31).

Broken families are deeply sad whether they break through necessity, circumstance or just plain sin. Today, hold them in your prayers, and yourself if you are part of such a family.

# A certain place

Imaginative

Read Genesis 28:10–22.

The well-known dream of Jacob's ladder occurs in 'a certain place' (v. 11 NRSV). Jacob seems to be on his own. Behind him lies his life so far: his family with its conflicts and struggle, joys and love. He has left the familiar, however broken, to journey to his uncle Laban to find a wife. Life is changing. But this night, worn out, he will rest in an 'in-between' place, between past and future where only this present moment lies. He lies down and rests his head on a stone.

Find a stone and hold it in your hand. What does it feel like? What might it be like to use a stone as a pillow? Think about times when you have moved from a comfortable to an uncomfortable place or experience. What was that like?

Reread Genesis 28:10–22 whilst holding your stone. As you read it, try to enter the dream as though you are there beside Jacob. Notice what you experience with your senses.

Jacob dreams and sees a ladder or ramp with angels ascending and descending on it.

How do the angels appear to you?

As God's messengers, what do you imagine they are taking into heaven?

What do you imagine that they bring down to earth?

The Lord stands beside Jacob. Imagine that God stands beside you now, experiencing what you experience. In Jacob's dream the Lord speaks promises to him. What do you experience God promising to you?

As Jacob wakes, he realises that this place, though hard and 'in-between', has become for him the place of encounter with God, a place where heaven and earth have touched for an instant. He knows that this moment and place of transition, though difficult, are awesome because they are the place where God dwells.

If you are in such an 'in-between' place now, or have ever been, offer your experience of that to God. Imagine him in that place with you. If you wish, write or draw your thoughts on paper and place your stone with them.

*God, you stand beside us in the 'in-between' and hard places of our lives, sometimes unnoticed, sometimes disregarded. Help us to know that whatever we think about you, you will always stand with us, waiting until the possible times when it is right to move on. Amen*

# A special place—making a ladder

## Creative

Find some bits and pieces with which to make a ladder. Almost anything might do. You could go for a walk and find some twigs or driftwood, or buy something from a hardware or craft store. Or you could make temporary use of some household objects such as wooden spoons, or even the back of a chair (especially if it already looks like a ladder), or you could cut out a ladder from a piece of paper. The key is to use something 'ordinary' to make something of greater significance.

Find a way to represent the angels. Try to make some distinction between the angels that are ascending and those which are descending.

With your completed ladder before you, think about times when you have hoped that your messages were taken up to heaven. Now remember occasions, if you can, when you felt people might have brought you messages from God.

Offer prayers of thanksgiving for times when God has redirected your feet or when you have sensed God in a change of life direction. If you write these prayers down, you could add them to the rungs of your 'ladder'. Luggage tags work well and you could make these yourself, again out of ordinary things found around the house.

Jacob marked the place of his dream with his stone pillow, which he anointed with oil as he renamed the place Bethel, God's house. As a final prayer, place the stone you used in 'A certain place', and the thoughts and prayers that went with it, next to your ladder. Rub oil on to the stone. Notice how the oil changes the appearance of the stone, usually bringing out fine detail you may not have noticed before. As you pray, ask God to reveal his presence to you in the tough places of your life.

# This place

## Creative/Going out

If you are able to access the internet, view the painting, *Christ Carrying the Cross* by Stanley Spencer, which is in the collection at Tate Britain.

Stanley Spencer was a 20th-century artist whose religious art sometimes paints Christ in the setting of his home village of Cookham in Berkshire. In this picture, Christ is carrying his cross through the streets of Cookham on his way to the crucifixion. Spend some time with the image. You may find you need to look really closely to identify Jesus himself. Notice the ladders in the painting which may provide a link to the passage about Jacob's dream.

What strikes you about the villagers, the occupants of the red-brick house, the other walkers on the road? Has anybody noticed Jesus' presence? Does there seem to be much interest in what is going on? Why do you think that might be? If you were in the picture, where would you be? What could you do to make Christ visible?

If you are unable to access the picture, think about those places which you visit frequently; if possible, you could actually go to them. Has there ever been a time in your life when those places have been transformed to reveal the presence of God? How did it change the way you think about that place? What might you do to point God out to others?

> *God of all life, you promise to be present with us and yet sometimes it is really hard to know that you are there. Help us to be aware of the signs of your presence and then inspire us by your Spirit to point others to them as well.*
> *Amen*

# Rachel

**Creative**

Read Genesis 29:1–14.

The story of how Jacob meets his wife-to-be Rachel follows immediately on from his dream at Bethel. The original passage in Hebrew literally begins, 'Jacob lifted up his feet and went…' We are not told how long his physical journey to the land of the East took, but coming up in the following chapters will be an even longer and more difficult personal and spiritual journey which, once again, will be filled with the recurrent themes of deceit, jealousy and favouritism.

In these 14 verses, the original hearers of the passage would have clearly recognised a betrothal narrative with its triple motif of wells, woman and man. Jacob rushes headlong into what he believes to be his destiny with Rachel. Note how he hurries to roll away the stone from the well and to water the flock in breach of the local custom, and then kisses Rachel before he has even introduced himself! There is a sense that Jacob feels his journey is over the minute he sees Rachel. But time and his plans are about to be slowed down and turned on their heads.

Laban, Rachel's father, has other ideas about how the story will continue and they involve making Jacob work as a servant to gain Rachel's hand and, through trickery, marrying Jacob to both his daughters. Jacob goes from favoured son to hireling, serving time for the woman he loves and being married by a trick to her sister

Leah in the process; read about this in chapters 29 and 30. As you read, take time to consider how Leah might have felt and God's provision for her.

Have you ever experienced a time when you thought life was slotting into place perfectly, only to find that plans became altered? Have there been times in life when you have looked back and realised that a passage of time or period of waiting was needed to appreciate God's right moment to answer prayer? Perhaps you are in the waiting time now.

Sometimes we start a journey with God full of hope and promise, only to find a much longer, more complex road in front of us.

Try drawing a path to represent your life. Pay particular note to places where the path turns in new directions and places where it has been even and level. Where are the places of change and where are the places you identify as times of waiting? From the perspective of hindsight, can you see God's hand at work in these places? Or are there times when you missed God's presence?

# Waiting and trusting

## Liturgy

This responsive exchange uses examples of waiting from the psalms to pray through those times when we wait with God.

*Lead me in your truth, and teach me, for you are the God of my salvation; for you I wait all day long. (Psalm 25:5 NRSV)*

**Guiding God, keep me faithful to your ways even when I can't see where the path is going. Help me to trust you on days when the journey with you feels stuck and unclear.**

*Wait for the Lord; be strong, and let your heart take courage; wait for the Lord! (Psalm 27:14)*

God, you uphold me; remind me that I am your beloved child on days when I feel low. Lord God, help me to trust in your timing, to know that it is perfect.

*Be still before the Lord, and wait patiently for him; do not fret over those who prosper in their way, over those who carry out evil devices. (Psalm 37:7)*

God of justice, I look around at the world and see its injustice. I don't understand it. Help me to trust you on days when life seems wrong and to pray for the day when your just and gentle rule will come.

*I wait for the Lord, my soul waits, and in his word I hope. (Psalm 130:5)*

God of hope, my soul longs for you and needs to believe your promises are true. Help me to put my hope in you always.

# A costly encounter

## Reflective

Read Genesis 32:1—33:12.

After the years with Laban, Jacob is now ready to return home, but knows he must seek reconciliation with his brother Esau. The last time we saw Esau he was threatening to kill Jacob and, as far as we know, there has been no contact between the brothers in the intervening 20 years.

As Jacob approaches their meeting, he sends messengers to Esau to tell of the wealth he has accumulated. On their return, they report that Esau is on his way with four hundred men. Jacob, fearing a fight, divides his company hoping that one part at least will survive. He then does something we have not seen much of—

he prays to God for deliverance before sending a substantial gift of cattle and goods to his brother. He leaves the camp to spend the night alone.

During the night, Jacob wrestles with an unknown opponent in a seemingly evenly matched struggle which lasts until daybreak. At the end, Jacob is a changed man. He receives a new name (Israel) which will lead to a new call and a blessing. However, he is also wounded: he will walk from now on with a limp. It is clear from the text that whoever the opponent is, Jacob believes he has, in some way, met God (32:30).

Have you ever met God as a result of struggle? At such times we may not recognise God's presence (just as we don't really know who Jacob's mysterious opponent is) but, looking back, we can discern the ways in which God was there.

Think back on a time of struggle. Was there any sense of the presence of God within it? If not, how did that feel? If so, can you now discern how God was there and in what form?

Such times in our lives rarely leave us untouched—we, like Jacob, are changed. Sometimes that change can be positive, a new calling or a blessing, and sometimes we can be wounded. Sometimes both blessing and wound are true. Give to God the good and the bad of your meetings with him.

*Wounded Jesus, on the cross you wrestled with evil, suffering and forgiveness all for love, all for me. Scarred Jesus, in your resurrection you released goodness, healing and eternal life, all for love, all for me. Help me today to come to you as I am and transform me in your love.*
*Amen*

# Reconciliation with Esau

## Imaginative/Creative

Read Genesis 33.

The sun rises and a new day dawns for Jacob, now limping and renamed; he looks up and sees his brother coming towards him. The moment of reckoning draws near.

Jacob now places himself between his beloved family and his brother and bows before him. I wonder if he was surprised by Esau's reaction. For, rather than the anticipated anger, Jacob finds himself embraced. As far as we can tell from the narrative, this is a first for the brothers who seem to have been in conflict since before birth. The initiative for this embrace comes from Esau who, though not without fault himself, had been cheated by his brother Jacob.

In this encounter Jacob had sought to buy favour from his brother, to protect his family and himself by offering his brother part of his amassed wealth. Esau, too, had come to the meeting with 400 men, clearly also concerned as to what he might find. Yet at the sight of each other, the years of struggle seem to disappear in a single act of reconciliation. There is no price one can put upon love freely given in this way. What Jacob discovered in Esau is an earthly imitation of the heavenly embrace waiting for us in God.

Find a cross or draw one on to a piece of paper. God's grace to us, which is expressed most clearly in the cross, cost God dearly and yet is given to us totally free. Imagine yourself coming to God and discovering the free love of his embrace. How does it feel? Rest in this moment for as long as you can, and let yourself be loved by God. When you are ready, place your cross next to the ladder you made earlier and leave it there as a reminder of the place where heaven is rooted to earth for us.

And finally ...

We leave our journey with Jacob at this point, but his story continues, interlaced with that of his most famous son, Joseph. Do take the time to find out what happens next and to discover that, although he has a new name and a new beginning, the old Jacob is still very much present. As you read, notice how God keeps faith with this family, bringing all things to good in the end.

*Loving God, help me to trust you through the twists and turns of life. May I seek you where you are, find you where I am and know your guiding presence in all things.*
*Amen*

# Clothes

*Sally Welch*

## Naked and ashamed

**Introduction/Bible study**

Read Genesis 2:25 and 3:6–7.

It is a common feeling amongst Christians that the clothes we wear are at best an irrelevance and at worst an invitation to pride and an indication that one has succumbed to the temptations of earthly life. 'Consider the lilies of the field,' we are reminded in Matthew 6:28 (NRSV). 'Do not worry, saying... what will we wear? For it is the Gentiles who strive for all these things' (vv. 31–32). A study of the Bible, however, reveals many different attitudes and uses of clothing, not all of which are worthy of condemnation.

We begin, naturally, at the beginning, with the story of how the innocence of Adam and Eve is corrupted by their bad choices and revealed by their sudden awareness of their nakedness. As soon as the fruit from the tree of the knowledge of good and evil is consumed, Adam and Eve regret their course of action. Their openness before the Lord is no longer free and unselfconscious; they must hide themselves in the hope that they will conceal the knowledge of their guilt from God. This is a fruitless exercise, however—God is already aware of their actions and deeply saddened by them. The consequence of their disobedience is immediate and unavoidable: freedom and leisure must be replaced by subjection to the demands of the soil and slavery to the seasons. Punished they must be, but they are not unloved, and God demonstrates this by replacing their makeshift garments with proper clothing. As we will see later on, items of clothing are presented as signs of office; they are symbols of status and dignity. Adam and Eve will have to face the harsh realities of life outside the garden of Eden, but they will do so wearing robes given to them by God as a promise of his continuing care for his children.

*Heavenly Father, when we feel unprotected against the forces of the world, help us to remember that you have clothed us with your love.*
*Amen*

# Joseph's robe

### Creative

Read Genesis 37:3–4.

Perhaps the most famous garment in the Bible, made more noteworthy by the Andrew Lloyd Webber musical *Joseph and the Amazing Technicolor Dreamcoat*, Jacob could not possibly have guessed the consequences of his gift to his favourite son. Given out of love for the young man and gratitude that he was born to him in his old age, Jacob little thought of the effect that such a demonstration of favouritism would have on his already envious older sons. It proved to be the catalyst for a series of events that would lead Joseph from slavery to status, then from imprisonment to great responsibility, culminating in Joseph saving his entire family from famine.

Few garments are glamorous enough to turn the wearer into a 'walking work of art', but clothing can be the holder of many memories. We know that Jacob wept over Joseph's robe, stained with the blood of a goat as 'proof' of his death. I wonder, did he keep it and, years later, weep for joy at the miraculous restoration of his son to him?

Have you ever kept a favourite piece of clothing—one of your own or one belonging to someone you love? Take it or a favoured item out and look at it once more. Remember when it was worn and who wore it. Thank God for the gifts of love remembered. Using a large piece of paper and some crayons, draw a single article of clothing—a shirt or jacket or robe like Joseph's. Divide it into squares like patchwork and fill each square with the colour or pattern of a garment that has meant something to you. Try and cover your life's experiences—from a favourite childhood coat, perhaps, to the clothes you wear today. As you colour them in, pray for the people you have shared your life with and thank God for their love.

# David dances

## Imaginative

Read 2 Samuel 6:12–15.

*It is a breathless, hot day, but the crowds waiting by the gates of the city do not disperse. After years of battle, of lives lost or damaged, of hardship and suffering, oppression and defeat, the Ark of the Covenant is being returned to Jerusalem—the tangible presence of God's promise to his people that he would never abandon them, and would always care for them.*

*Finally, faintly, the sound of trumpets, of tambourines, of singing is heard. The crowd scan the horizon, seeking the first glimpse of the procession. As it gradually becomes visible the excitement changes first to surprise, then astonishment. The King, David, is heading up the procession—as he indeed should—but he is not walking with dignity, robed in heavy silk clothing indicative of the high nobility of his office. No, he is clad only in a length of cloth wrapped around his trunk—just enough to satisfy the demands of modesty—and he is dancing!*

For David's God was not one who needed to be protected and surrounded by solemnity. David's God was one who had ventured with him into the most difficult and dangerous situations. David's God had supported and encouraged him when he was frightened and lonely, when his enemies surrounded him. It was to this God that David had poured out his hopes and fears, his anger and triumphs, and it was this God that David worshipped, not with a self-conscious awareness of the dignity of his position, but with his whole heart, body and soul together in one glorious act of praise.

How does it feel to praise God with your whole self? Why not play some praise music, shed your inhibitions and dance! If you don't feel joyful, move in a way that reflects your feelings towards God right now.

# Make the ephod of gold

## Spotlight

Read Exodus 28:1–14.

From the earliest times, those who were appointed to serve in the house of the Lord wore clothing to distinguish themselves from others. Garments of the finest possible weave, with the richest available threads, were put on prior to leading the rituals which composed the worship of the Hebrews. This practice did not continue unbroken into Christian times, as it was initially believed that the coming of the kingdom of God was so imminent that very little in the way of new clothing was required at all. During the time of the persecution of Christians, distinctive clothing would have been dangerous, so it was not until the third century that the offices of bishop, priest and deacon had identifiably specific clothing assigned to them. However, by the end of the fifth century the garments of bishops, priests and deacons had become fixed and distinctive.

There are many reasons for this distinction in dress—for some, the putting on of separate, fine garments is a declaration that the act of worship is distinct from everyday life, that to present oneself before God, particularly in a leadership role, is such a privilege that it must be marked out by extra-fine clothes, robes set aside for that purpose and for no other. Others find that the donning of a particular cut and style of clothing renders the wearer's personality almost invisible, so that it does not act as a barrier between those who are being led and their relationship with God. A sense of the universality of the Church, of people throughout the world gathering for the same purpose, led in the same acts of praise and thanksgiving, is given weight by the similarity in appearance of the worship leaders. Others, however, feel that distinctions between clergy and congregation are divisive and unnecessary, leading to false dignity being accorded to those in leadership.

How do the clothes you wear reflect your personality? Look at your three favourite garments—what do you think they say about you?

# Everyone who came brought a gift

## Bible study

Read 1 Kings 10:23–25.

The rise and fall of Solomon is a tragic tale of a fine and worthy human being corrupted by the things of the world, until the damage to his personality prevented him from carrying out his original purpose. His story is a stern warning to all those who allow themselves to be seduced by success, drawn into believing that the external manifestations of power (wealth and influence) are more important than the necessity to live righteously before the one in whose hands true power lies.

In the beginning, Solomon's character—his truthfulness, humility and earnest desire to serve his people—was a delight to God. Famously offered a choice between wealth and wisdom, on choosing wisdom, Solomon was rewarded with wealth as well, but in this wealth lay his undoing. He was given the privilege of building the temple to God in Jerusalem, a privilege not accorded even to David. His judgement was sought throughout the world, but those who received his insights gave great treasures in return, and gradually the charms of gold and silver, and the attractions of the many wives Solomon took, led him away from the right path.

We must take care that we too learn to accord the good things of this world their proper place. We are able to delight in them because they are part of God's creation, but we should not allow longing for them to corrupt us. We must keep clear the paths between us and God, keep the ways open between us and our neighbour, never permitting the selfish accumulation of possessions to overwhelm us or distract us from our true purpose in life. 'Articles of silver and gold, robes, weapons and spices' (v. 25 NIV) become tainted and spoilt when those around us do not have enough to eat; better still that all should be able to rejoice in God's gifts.

How many 'designer' or expensive garments do you own? Why did you buy them? Could you have spent the money differently?

# Fairtrade clothing

## Spotlight

Read Isaiah 58:6–7.

On 24 April 2013 in Dhaka, Bangladesh, an eight-storey factory building called Rana Plaza collapsed. Approximately 2500 people were injured and over 1100 killed in the biggest garment factory accident in history. The collapse of this building and the terrible consequences were the direct result of a corrupt and greedy manufacturing system, where the determination to cut production costs and increase revenue was greater than any concern for the lives of the workers who spent many hours in squalid conditions, working for a miserable amount of money.

The scale of this tragedy brought to the surface the iniquitous conditions under which many clothes are manufactured at such high cost to the workers and their families, so that the over-privileged consumer can indulge their taste for low-cost garments which are worn only a few times before they are discarded in favour of the latest fashions. More and more people are questioning such practices and demanding from clothing manufacturers a responsible attitude towards their workers, ensuring safe and healthy working conditions and fair pay.

By shopping ethically, by paying attention to the way in which our clothing is made, we can reach out to our fellow human beings, ensuring that they can live and work safely and productively. By buying fairly traded clothes from the many companies that now supply them, we can challenge unfair trading practices and support approaches to trade which promote sustainable production and help developing countries transform the lives of their citizens.

This is not a cost-free exercise—fairly traded clothes, manufactured in safe conditions by workers paid a living wage with access to health provision and education will cost significantly more than those sold in their thousands into high street stores throughout our country. But we can wear them knowing that, by doing so, we are loving our neighbour in practical, transformational ways that honour both them and God. The next time you buy a piece of clothing, try to identify where it came from, and who made it. Is it available from a Fairtrade producer?

# Dressed and in his right mind

## Meditative

Read Luke 8:26–27.

For many years the man had lived on the outskirts of the town, amongst the tombs and graves that heralded the hinterland, the place of uncleanness, the place of exile. Something should have been done about him, but when the demons were upon him, he was too strong for the people of the town—they had tried to restrain him but he had broken free each time, wrenching the shackles which bound him out of their mooring and roaring and raving at the onlookers in his madness. He wore no clothes—a further offence against propriety and decency, a statement in itself that he lay outside the boundaries of normal life. But for all that, he had found a place in the structure of the town; everyone knew the areas he inhabited and what to expect from him. Even in his wildest moments there was a sort of continuity, of stability.

That is, until the arrival of the strange prophet, who refused the hospitality of the great and the good, choosing instead to spend his time amongst the outcast and exiles of the places he visited. The people of the town had been waiting for his arrival, eager to hear news from other parts of the country, to listen to new stories, meet travellers and exchange gossip. But this man had not behaved as other visitors; he had not visited the temple or approached the elders of the town. Instead he had made his way to the cemetery, to the lair of the wild one, the one haunted by demons. The townspeople rushed to witness the event, hoping perhaps for a dramatic encounter, maybe with some violence. Instead, they found the madman and the prophet in quiet conversation, seated amongst the tombstones. No longer naked and raving, the man was 'dressed and in his right mind' (v. 35), able once again to take his place amongst the citizenry of the town, an outcast no more.

Try wearing a garment the wrong way round—take off your cardigan or sweater and put it on back to front. Put your shoes on the wrong feet, or simply unbutton a garment that you usually wear fastened. Spend some time reflecting on how this feels. Are you uncomfortable? Do you feel ill at ease? Does this feeling extend to your mind as well as your body? Does your relationship with God and the people around you sometimes feel like this? Now put things back so that they feel comfortable again. What would it take to make your prayer life feel like this? How might you improve your relationships with those around you so that they too can feel 'right'?

# Seek his kingdom

## Going out

Read Luke 12:22–31.

This well-known passage is a love song to God's creation. Luke invites us to glory in the works of God's hand, taking note of every detail lovingly completed in its infinite beauty. If this is how God lingers over every tiny insect, blossom, creature, how much more, declares Luke, will God care for us, his children!

And so we can play our part too in caring for our surroundings, nurturing and tending our natural world so that it can sing its full song of praise to its creator, every note unblemished, giving brightness and depth to the chords of glory.

As we go about our daily round, in city, town or country, we can be God's gardeners. Even if a garden is not available to us, the smallest plot or even windowsill can be cultivated to produce flowers or vegetables. Should even this not be possible, then opportunities exist for action within the wider community. The railway station of the country town in which I live has the most beautiful flowerbeds, lovingly tended by a small group of volunteers, the glorious results of whose diligence and energy bring joy to all who pass by on the busy line. The churchyard is monitored by another group, who undertake the regular tasks of litter picking, weeding and edging, all of which add to the welcome and peace of the place.

Although we may not be in a position to take on such commitments, we can still be alert to our surroundings: pausing to pick up litter and place it in a bin, taking five minutes to remove the weeds from a public place, acknowledging in each act our individual responsibility for our communal spaces, revealing beauty where it has been hidden by the ugliness of a disdain for nature, allowing God's glory its full expression.

# Learning Knights

## Spotlight

Read John 13:34–35.

In 1902, after much prayer and consideration, a young woman by the name of Beatrice Hankey formed the Blue Pilgrims. Organised and led by women, the group met to study the Bible and go out to serve people in need. These simple principles, embodied in the phrase 'by love, serve', provided the foundation for their calling. Making use of the Anglo-Saxon translation of disciples as 'learning knights', and modelling their community on Arthur and the Knights of the Round Table, members took upon themselves new names which indicated both their challenges and their aims. (Beatrice herself was known as Help.) Meetings were known as Camelots, and programmes of service as Quests.

The Blue Pilgrims have met times of need with active, practical help, setting up 'Home Huts' in World War I, offering aid during the Depression, rescuing refugees during World War II and working for reconciliation in its aftermath and during times of political unrest in Northern Ireland. The choice of clothing of the original founders inspired their name: 'A blue and white frock, plain, or blue coat and skirt, a blue headdress, a bag with stole, a knapsack and a light mac and umbrella.' Thus, like nuns and nurses, doctors and emergency workers, the Blue Pilgrims became recognised in the areas where they worked as people in whom one could trust, and also those in whom the love of God was manifest. Far from being indicators of status or manifestations of wealth, their garments became declarations of faith and of the principle of loving service.

Today, the Blue Pilgrims still hold regular Camelots, gathering together for fellowship and prayer, resourcing each other for their work and service in the wider community. Still led by women, the Camelots are noted for their lack of hierarchy, their hospitality and welcome and the rest and relaxation they offer to their members.

What uniforms do you wear? These may not be obvious; consider uniforms such as aprons for hospitality or overalls when helping out a friend. How do they make you feel? Do you hide behind your 'uniform' or does it give you extra authority?

# Freely you have received; freely give

### Creative

Read Matthew 10:5–10.

What courage is required to be a disciple! Jesus is sending these men out to preach a radical new message, one which will undoubtedly inflame the anger of those who maintain the status quo. He is sending them for an unspecified time, to unknown places, to share their lives with strangers. To crown all this, they are not even allowed to surround themselves with the security of extra belongings; they must make the journey relying on God, not themselves, relying on the hospitality of those they meet along the way.

In what ways do we try to counterbalance our fear of the future by surrounding ourselves with comfort objects? Just as children cling to teddy bears when they are lonely or afraid, so we often buy things to protect ourselves from unknown threats, clinging selfishly to goods which could be better used by others in greater need.

Jesus forbids his disciples from taking even a change of clothing; we can allow ourselves more than that, but it can be very liberating to 'pray through the wardrobe'. Open your wardrobe and cupboard doors, and ask God for the blessing of generosity and a spirit of unselfishness. Sort out those clothes which you no longer need; be ruthless over which you no longer wear. Take your unnecessary garments to a charity shop or sell them and give the money away. Feel how liberating it is to live uncluttered by possessions!

Just as we are released from the burden of caring for our surplus clothes, so Jesus promises us that we need no longer feel burdened by fear of the future; we simply need to put our trust in the one who holds the future.

I don't know what the future holds, but I know who holds the future…

# A scarlet robe

## Bible study

Read Matthew 27:27–31.

Clothing is a symbol of power, not only in the type of cloth it is made from, but in the style and even the colour. In cultures across the globe, men and women have been permitted or prevented from wearing certain items or colours of clothing as a way of marking them out. In biblical times, scarlet was the colour of royalty, a symbol of power. It was to be worn by only the top echelons of society. Here, however, the scarlet robe becomes an instrument of contempt. First of all, Jesus has his own clothes stripped from him in an attempt to deprive him of his individuality, his dignity.

This will not work, however, for Jesus finds his security not in mere externals, but in a relationship with God.

The offences do not stop there. In a gesture which contrasts the actions of God at the beginning of creation, when he robed Adam and Eve before he expelled them from the garden of Eden as a sign of his continuing love and support, here the Innocent One, who has committed no sin, is clothed by those who mean him harm. In this, Jesus stands side by side with all those who have been forced to wear clothes as a sign of inferior status—the loincloths of slaves, the dunce's cap of Victorian schooldays, the star of David by the Jewish people under the Nazi regime. But in this too, Jesus redeems all those who have suffered in this way, depriving the gesture of its power by the very nature of the one who allows it.

Let us not build our attitude to others upon the shallow foundations of what they look like or how they dress. Let us look instead beneath the outer shell to find the substance beneath. Find a picture or image of a powerful person—would you know they were important by what they wear? How do we make others feel less important by imposing clothing restrictions on them—prisoners, for example?

# He who overcomes

## Reflective

Read Revelation 3:5.

As we reflect on the many references made in the Bible to the clothes we wear, we can marvel that a simple garment can be capable of so many different interpretations. We see that clothing can be worn to set people apart, either for good as in the garments of priests which serve to remind all who see them of the holy nature of their task, or for evil as in the stripping and robing of Christ in the garments of mockery and contempt. We notice that what we wear should be taken seriously—we are reminded not to be overly preoccupied with the grandeur and style of articles, which are only outer coverings, but to be mindful of the method of their production and aware always of the needs of others and our responsibility towards them.

Garments are given as signs of love and respect, to be treasured and valued: gifts which honour the giver and the recipient. We can rejoice in the part we can play in God's creative work, appreciating the wide variety and uses of the clothes we wear. And always we look forward to the time when the things of this world will be redeemed and we will gather as children of God, 'dressed in white', around the throne of the King of Love himself.

*'See, I am coming soon; my reward is with me, to repay according to everyone's work. I am the Alpha and the Omega, the first and the last, the beginning and the end.' Blessed are those who wash their robes, so that they will have the right to the tree of life and may enter the city by the gates.*

REVELATION 22:12–14 NRSV

# Mary, Martha and Lazarus

*Helen Julian CSF*

## Mary, Martha and Lazarus

### Introduction

Mary, Martha and Lazarus are intriguing characters. They appear only three times in the Gospels, but each story is resonant and rich.

In Luke 10:38–42 we have the brief but very well-known story of Jesus visiting what is described as Martha's home. She complains that her sister Mary is sitting at Jesus' feet, and not helping to prepare the meal. The complaint elicits Jesus' famous words about Mary having chosen the better part. Lazarus doesn't feature in this story at all.

Then there are two stories in John's Gospel. In 11:1–44 there is the raising of Lazarus. Although Lazarus is the subject of the story, it is Martha who is most active as the story unfolds, and who makes a confession of faith comparable to that of Peter in Matthew 16:16. Almost immediately there is the third and final story, in John 12:1–8. Jesus again comes to join in a meal at the home of Mary, Martha and Lazarus (now identified as the home of Lazarus). This time Mary takes centre stage, anointing Jesus' feet with costly perfume, and wiping them with her hair.

In the Gospels, women often have only walk-on and silent roles, but of these three it is Lazarus who never speaks, while both Mary and Martha say and do significant things, and spark important teaching from Jesus.

After the third story, the trio disappear from the Gospels, though they have a rich afterlife in stories written later, which take them variously to Cyprus and to the south of France. It seems that the early Christians weren't satisfied with just the Gospel stories and wanted to know 'what happened next'.

Other Gospel stories have become attached to Mary too, both those of other women named Mary, and of other women who anoint Jesus; and in some of the later stories she is also conflated with Mary Magdalene.

Reflect on what you already know of Mary, Martha and Lazarus. What thoughts and feelings are sparked off by their stories? Do you think that you would have liked them, wanted to spend time with them in their home? You might like to write down your thoughts, and then return to them at the end of these readings to see what has changed.

# An alternative family

Reflective/Creative

'Friends are the new family' has become something of a cliché. The reality is that families and family relationships have always been very varied, and perhaps more so now than in the past, when the nuclear family of parents and their children was almost the only acceptable model. That is of course changing now, with blended families, single parents and new forms of partnership and marriage.

Martha, Mary and Lazarus are also a family: a family of siblings. And this household of two sisters and their brother seems to have been a place in which Jesus felt very much at home. Their home at Bethany, not far from Jerusalem, was somewhere Jesus obviously felt he could visit when he was passing, and be sure of a welcome. Perhaps it also provided a brief refuge from the crowds.

Jesus himself was of course not married, which was very unusual in his day and culture, and perhaps this is part of why he felt at home with these three. However welcoming couples are to their single friends, it can be hard not to feel the odd one out, painfully reminded of what may feel lacking in the life of the single person, especially if that singleness has not been chosen.

The Church often describes itself as a family, and this can be a strength. But families are not always wonderful places, and sometimes the Church reflects the darker side of family life as well as its love and support. In their eagerness to make families welcome and included, churches risk sidelining the single—whether simply unmarried, or divorced or widowed. I wonder whether Jesus found affirmation of his own choice in the household at Bethany?

Sit quietly, and reflect on your own experience of family—your family of origin, and whatever family you now find yourself part of, whether that is of blood or of friendship or the family of Church. Draw this family and notice where you place Jesus within the family. What might he say to you, and to other family members? If this brings up painful memories, ask Jesus to heal them. If there are happy memories, give thanks for them.

# What's in a name?

## Reflective/Creative

There is a lady in my community with whom I'm quite regularly confused, and the same happens to her. We're about the same height and of similar colouring, but apart from that we can't see any reason for the confusion. But people can be quite definite that they've met me doing something—preaching, leading a Quiet Day— even when I can say categorically that I've never been to that place.

It's a strange feeling to have your identity doubted in this way. Mary of Bethany has suffered more than most over the centuries.

From Gregory the Great (who was pope in the sixth century) onwards, most people put together various Gospel women named Mary, and various women who anointed Jesus, into one composite 'Mary'. It wasn't until 1969 that this confusion was unpicked in the Roman Catholic Church and each woman, named and unnamed, given back her own identity and story.

Is this something which has happened to you? How did it feel? Were you annoyed, intrigued, hurt—or perhaps happy to be taken for someone you admire? And more particularly, what does your name mean to you? Do you know why you were given it? Perhaps it's been a family name for generations, or was your mother's favourite film star. Have you kept it as it was, or chosen to shorten it, use a nickname or even change it altogether? What name does God know you by?

If you were to change your name, what would your new name be? A new name can be a powerful mark of a new beginning, a change in your way of life.

Take one of your names and draw it in large empty letters on a piece of paper. Decorate it to reflect the person it names. As you do this, offer it to God and invite him to show you hidden aspects of your name and self.

## Mary as disciple

### Meditative

Start today by reading Luke 10:38–42. Do it as a form of *lectio divina*—read it slowly, and pause to allow it to sink in. Read it again, and then pause again. Does any particular word or phrase resonate for you? If so, spend time simply savouring it, turning it over in your heart, waiting for what it has to offer you.

This is a kind of parallel to what Mary was doing sitting at Jesus' feet. Sitting at someone's feet is often seen and taught as a model of the contemplative life, and we'll be looking at that later. But it's also the place of a disciple or student of a rabbi. The classical relationship of rabbi and student was not one of a weekly session in a classroom, perhaps with an occasional one-to-one meeting to discuss a piece of work. The student went to live in the rabbi's house, and learnt as much from what he (and it was normally he) saw of how the rabbi lived as from formal teaching, though that did also take place.

So Mary, in sitting at Jesus' feet, was doing something quite radical. Opinion varies as to quite how radical—was it unheard of for women to learn the Torah, or just unusual? It was at least the latter, and perhaps this is part of why Martha is so put out; not only is Mary leaving her to do all the work, she's also doing something out of the ordinary.

Think back over all your teachers—whether in school, in a sport, in some other skill or simply in life. Who is the one who taught you the most, who was the most important for you? Reflect on what you learnt, and whether some of that was from how the teacher was, as much as from what they taught. Then write a letter to this teacher, telling them what you remember, what you learnt from them, and expressing your gratitude. Be aware that sometimes we learn best from difficult and demanding teachers.

## Confessing the faith

### Bible reading

Begin by reading John 11:1–44, focusing on the role of Martha in the story. You will notice that although this is always called 'the raising of Lazarus', and that is indeed the climax of the story, at its heart, in central place, is the dialogue of Martha and Jesus.

Martha takes the initiative, going out to meet Jesus, and is bold enough to complain that he has taken so long to arrive. But she also expresses her belief that Jesus can turn around even this desperate situation. Jesus takes the belief she already has in a final resurrection, and uses it to elicit one of the most striking confessions of faith in all the gospels: 'You are the Messiah, the Son of God' (v. 27 NRSV), Martha declares, a confession paralleled only by Peter in Matthew 16:16. Some churches have a feast celebrating 'the confession of Peter' but Martha's identical recognition of Jesus' true identity is far less well known and rarely celebrated.

It's noteworthy that her confession comes not as a response to Lazarus' resurrection, but in the dialogue with Jesus. Martha too is taught by the Lord, as Mary was. Her way of engaging and learning is different, but Jesus responds no less fully.

With the mark of a true apostle, Martha immediately goes to 'call' another—her sister Mary, just as Andrew and Philip called Peter and Nathanael (John 1:40–47). And the words of Martha's confession are used again in John 20:31, a verse summing up the purpose of the whole Gospel.

This is a different picture of Martha than the discontented housewife in Luke, and worth holding together with it. Perhaps it makes getting to know her better rather more attractive?

## Mary the contemplative

### Reflective

If we think of contemplation, of being contemplative, we probably think of sitting still, with our eyes closed, thinking of nothing, or perhaps having only holy thoughts. This is certainly one way of expressing this dimension, but it isn't the only one. For many people it isn't the best one, or even a possible one.

If we think of Mary as an example of contemplation, we see that even she wasn't in fact doing this—she was sitting still, but she was listening to Jesus as he talked. She was giving all her attention to him and to his words, and that can be a clue for us. To be contemplative, we need to give all our attention to what we are doing. This has always been difficult, but is probably even more difficult today, with so many distractions readily available. Strengthening the contemplative dimension means making choices: not automatically turning on music or the radio, staying offline for part of each day, deliberately choosing what we read or listen to, saying no to some things so that we can say yes to what we most deeply desire.

This opens up space for contemplative moments; for noticing the first star as the sky darkens; for being drawn into prayer for a friend whose needs have come to mind; for appreciating the first sip of coffee. These may then give us the taste for longer periods of attention, whether that is listening to a talk by a favourite speaker, or to music which draws us to God, reading slowly and meditatively, walking attentively and mindfully, or simply sitting in God's presence. But in each case we do this with all our attention, doing just the thing we are doing. For a time, we step away from 'being worried and distracted by many things' (Luke 10:41). And perhaps we discover that the world does not fall apart, and that we return to our active tasks refreshed and energised.

What stops you being more contemplative today?

What are you going to do when you have finished praying? Whatever it is, do it with your full attention. Notice what you are doing. Be aware of how things feel and what you hear and see. Notice where God is as you continue your life.

# Being Lazarus

## Imaginative

If you are able, lie down on the floor. If you can't, sit in a chair where you will be able to stay very still. You are Lazarus in his tomb.

Feel the stillness of death, and the binding around your hands and feet and head. Experience the lack of light and warmth and sound, staying with the experience for several minutes.

What in your present life is deadening? What makes you feel bound and unable to move?

You begin to hear sound outside the tomb. People are gathering. Perhaps you recognise a voice or two. Then there is a grating sound, and the stone at the tomb entrance is heaved aside. Light penetrates the darkness, and the voices become louder.

You hear Jesus speaking, and strain to hear his words.

What do you imagine he is saying?

Then you hear him clearly using your name and calling to you, 'Come out!' What feelings does that evoke? Joy? Disbelief? The impossibility of it?

But slowly you begin to move, stumbling towards the faint light. As you emerge, you hear Jesus saying, 'Unbind him/her, and let him/her go.'

Who unbinds the cloths around you? What is the first thing you see, touch, smell, as life is restored to you? What do you say to your family? What do you say to Jesus? How does this experience change you?

This meditation may evoke strong feelings; you might want to write down what you experience so that you can continue to pray with it, and perhaps share it with a trusted friend or guide.

## Another meal at Bethany

### Imaginative

In John 12:1–8, there is a second meal at the house in Bethany, with these three whom Jesus loved (John 11:5). The atmosphere is different to that in Luke, though the characters of the two sisters are recognisably the same. Martha serves, and Mary is once again at Jesus' feet. Given its place in the Gospel, this is likely to have been a meal in gratitude and thanksgiving for the raising of Lazarus.

But there are deeper currents too. The two sisters are the ministers of a supper which takes place on a Sunday evening, the day on which the early Church would go on to celebrate the Eucharist. Mary's anointing of Jesus' feet may bring to your mind Jesus' washing of the disciples' feet at the Last Supper, which will happen in a few days' time. In both of these stories, Judas features as the image of a false disciple. Is there a contrast here with Mary, the image of the true disciple? The relationship between Mary and Martha seems more harmonious. Perhaps now the two sisters are content with their roles, and able to see them as God-given and God-valued.

And what of Lazarus? He says nothing, but he is at the table with Jesus. Perhaps he was still trying to make sense of what had happened to him.

Read through this story slowly. Can you imagine yourself in the house at the meal? Who are you? Perhaps you are one of the main characters, or maybe you are another guest, or a servant, looking on as this scene plays out. Jesus speaks; who does he speak to and what does he say? Then he speaks to you—listen and, if you can, respond. Stay at this meal for as long as you wish.

## Choosing the better part?

### Creative

What did Jesus mean when he said that Mary had 'chosen the better part' (Luke 10:42 NRSV)? The traditional interpretation is that he valued the contemplative life over the active. This was often explained as being because the work of active service was necessary now, but would end with this life, while the work of contemplation would continue into the life of heaven. So Mary was preparing now for eternal life.

A few commentators doubt that Mary had chosen the better part. For them, Martha was the example of the mature Christian, while Mary was at an earlier stage which she would eventually have to move beyond. Meister Eckhart, an early fourteenth-century Dominican, and Bultmann, a German theologian of the twentieth century, both held this view.

I find Aelred of Rievaulx has one of the best understandings of this passage. He talks about both Martha and Mary living under the one roof, both pleasing and acceptable to the Lord, and loved by him. Therefore, he concludes, they should never be separated; and in our lives, both dimensions—the active and the contemplative—are necessary and good.

Our lives are lived on a continuum between the active and contemplative poles, and we will find ourselves at different places on it as our life moves on and changes. Take a sheet of paper and draw this continuum; then represent along it (in symbols, words, colours) what draws you to either end. Sit and reflect on what you've produced, and prayerfully decide where you are on the continuum at present. Then consider where you would ideally like to be (the centre is not necessarily the ideal position). How might you move nearer to your ideal? Can you identify one thing you can do this week which would help this move?

# Fan fiction

### Creative

Mary, Martha and Lazarus have a rich life beyond the Gospels. Two main sets of stories take them to different parts of the world. In the Orthodox tradition, Lazarus and Martha flee Jerusalem after the martyrdom of Stephen, while Mary stays with John the Apostle in

Jerusalem. Later, they all travel to Cyprus, where Lazarus becomes the first bishop of Kittim, now Larnaca, and all three die on the island. As late as AD890, there was a tomb on the island with the inscription, 'Lazarus the friend of Christ'.

A much later legend in the 13th century has all three leaving Judea around AD48, and sailing to Provence, where they preached and converted the people. By this time, Mary has lost her separate identity and has 'become' Mary Magdalene. Lazarus becomes bishop of Marseilles. By the 13th century his relics had indeed moved, via Constantinople, to Marseilles, so this story could be intended to account for their presence.

In this legend, Martha stayed in Provence, and had an interesting encounter with a dragon, which we'll look at separately. She's also celebrated in the Spanish town of Villajoyosa, where she's believed to have saved the town, in 1538, from an attack by pirates by causing a flash flood which wiped them out.

Who in the Bible intrigues you? Whose story frustrates you by ending too soon? Pick a biblical character—it may be one of Mary, Martha and Lazarus, or someone else—and write an imagined story of their life after the biblical story ends.

# Martha and the dragon

### Story

*In the river Rhone, as it passed through a wood between Arles and Avignon, lived a great monster, the Tarasque. It is described as a dragon, half beast and half fish, bigger than an ox or a horse, with sword-sharp teeth, and horns and wings. It was as strong as twelve lions or bears. The dragon lurked in the river, killing passers-by, and capsizing ships. Even the dragon's dung was deadly, and burnt up anything it touched.*

*The local people appealed to Martha to save them from the dragon, and she responded to their cry for help. Carrying a cross, she set out for the wood, and found the dragon eating a man. She sprinkled the dragon with holy water, and showed him the cross, and the dragon became tame—tame enough for her to place her sash around its neck and lead it back to the village.*

*The people dedicated their church to St Martha in honour of her great feat, and her relics are still believed to lie in the church in Tarascon.*

Are there dragons in your life, lurking in dark places and destroying life? How might you follow the example of Martha in taming the dragon without violence?

# Friends of God

## Liturgy

Pray this litany slowly and reflectively as a way of looking back on our theme. It may spark your own prayers too.

*Mary, Martha and Lazarus, you were loved by Jesus. May I also know myself to be loved by God.*

*Mary, Martha and Lazarus, you welcomed Jesus into your home, gave him food and listened to his word. May I also welcome him into my home and listen to his words to me.*

*Martha, you served with energy and commitment. May I serve in the same way, without resentment.*

*Mary, you sat at Jesus' feet and learnt from him. May I learn how to stop, to sit with Jesus and allow him to teach me.*

*Lazarus, you were given back your life at the word of God. May I believe in the power of resurrection in my own life.*

*Mary, you were unashamed of your love for Jesus. May I express my love in extravagant gestures and simple service.*

*Mary, Martha and Lazarus, you have been remembered through the centuries as friends of God. May I follow your examples to live out my own calling as a friend of God.*
*Amen*

# Evelyn Underhill

*Sue McCoulough*

## Who was Evelyn Underhill?

### Introduction

Nestling in the Essex countryside lies Pleshey, an ancient settlement adorned by colourful stuccoed houses. In medieval times it was famed for its castle and estates, but the village's importance diminished. It became renowned again in the early 20th century, as a centre for spiritual growth. Remarkably for that time, much was due to the efforts of a woman, Evelyn Underhill (1875–1941).

Underhill first went to the Retreat House, Pleshey, as it came to be known, in 1922. From then until her death, she contributed hugely to life there and at other retreat houses. Her intelligent, common-sense approach helped lay people develop their spiritual life beyond saying routine prayers and attending church on Sundays. Until then, in Britain at least, only clergymen or inhabitants of religious houses experienced the privilege of spending 'time apart' with God.

Evelyn Underhill's writing, teaching and spiritual direction were rooted in a deep spiritual vision that branched out to address thorny practical questions. How could ordinary people, living in an increasingly hectic and unstable world, integrate and grow their spiritual life with God? Underhill herself moved from an early agnosticism to an intellectual belief in a wholly transcendent God. Over time, she embraced the message of the Gospels but struggled to settle in a church. Eventually her dilemmas strengthened her ability to reach out to people battling with religious and denominational uncertainties. Once settled in the Church of England, she helped Protestants enjoy the legacy of Catholic

75

mystics. She relished God's grace in giving her a new, wholehearted faith in Christ, as both human and divine saviour of humanity. Later, Underhill shared her insights about the sacramental life within different Christian denominations. She claimed all had value, thus promoting modern ideas of ecumenism.

Think about your own spiritual journey so far. Have your beliefs and their expression changed much? Have there been external circumstances in your life or the world which have reshaped your faith over time? Perhaps a glance at old photos will remind you of different stages in your life, or you may have diaries depicting periods or events in your life. Note and pray with any findings.

## The Spiritual Life

### Reflective

There is no real occasion for tumult, strain, conflict, anxiety, once we have reached the living conviction that God is All…
Our spiritual life is His affair; because whatever we may think to the contrary, it is really produced by His steady attraction, and our humble and self-forgetful response to it. It consists in being drawn, at His pace and in His way, to the place where He wants us to be, not the place we fancied for ourselves.

From *The Spiritual Life* by Evelyn Underhill (1937)

Underhill's Christian commitment grew under guidance from her Roman Catholic spiritual director, Baron von Hügel (1852–1925). Seeing her love of Italian churches and Catholic forms of worship, he encouraged her to place Jesus Christ at the heart of her reflections. Perceptively, he saw also her desire for intellectual freedom. Von Hügel insisted she focus on practical works, claiming, 'There is too much blood in your head, visiting the poor will disperse it.'

Already busy with charitable and social engagements, Underhill wrote nearly 40 books, as well as many book reviews, novels, poems, pamphlets, broadcast talks and retreat addresses. *Mysticism*, written in her pre-Christian days, is still considered a classic in its field, seeking to address a popular Christian misconception that mysticism was only for saints or oddballs.

In *Concerning the Inner Life*, Underhill writes that the saints

are specialists… in a career to which all Christians are called… as that real life, that interior union with God grows, so does the saints' self-identification with humanity grow. They do not stand aside wrapped in delightful prayers… They go right down into the mess; and there right down in the mess, they are able to radiate God because they possess him.

Spend time thinking about any 'saint' who particularly inspires you, perhaps as much for their practical interaction with the world as their holiness. Does this influence your own practical service or prayer life in your community or church?

## *Immanence* and incarnation

### Poetry/Going out

Read Matthew 18:1–6.

*I come in the little things,*
*Saith the Lord:*
*Yea, on the glancing wings*
*Of eager birds, the softly pattering feet*
*Of furred and gentle beasts, I come to meet*
*Your hard and wayward heart. In brown, bright eyes*
*That peek from out the brake I stand confest.*

> *I come in the little things*
> *Saith the Lord:*
> *My starry wings*
> *I do forsake,*
> *Love's highway of humility to take:*
> *Meekly I fit my stature to your need.*
> *In beggar's part*
> *About your gates I shall not cease to plead—*
> *As man, to speak with man—*
> *Till by such art*
> *I shall achieve My Immemorial Plan,*
> *Pass the low lintel of the human heart.*

From *Immanence* by Evelyn Underhill (1937)

Underhill wanted to see her spiritual experience of an impersonal 'Reality' (her term for God) transformed to embrace a personal relationship with an incarnate, fully human God. Jesus' life was rooted in humility and total trust in his heavenly Father. He valued the small things of creation, arguing we should become like little children, trustfully depending on our heavenly parent to provide necessary good things.

If possible, go outside to discover 'the little things' that speak to you. Gardens in November can be full of berries; in the herb garden at Pleshey, sage, marjoram, thyme and mint still smell fragrant. As the trees grow bare and natural activity diminishes, what 'details' in your world particularly strike you? Notice especially vulnerable, fragile things that may not survive the ravages of winter. Pray for 'little' things: any vulnerable group, especially children, who concern you.

# Plunging into water

## Going out

Read 2 Timothy 1:3–13.

> Real prayer begins with the plunge into the water.

From Evelyn Underhill's 1928 retreat entitled *The Call of God*

For Evelyn Underhill, healthy spirituality involved taking risks: Christian life was based on trust, not on seeking a life of constant comfort.

Any searching and growth hinged on developing perseverance; thus she writes in *Worship*: 'a deep realism as regards human imperfection and sin, and also human suffering and struggle, is at the very heart of the Christian response to God; which, if it is to tally with the Christian revelation of disinterested love as summed up on the Cross, must include the element of hardness, cost and willing pain.'

Recall times when you resisted being taken out of your spiritual comfort zone. Are there other moments when, after prayer, you've taken a plunge into the water of faith and trust, despite fears for safety? Perhaps you have gone into the 'deep end' and risked drowning? How might you better anchor yourself deeply into Christ's care or be carried along by his currents, despite initial discomfort?

Today, go to a swimming pool or the sea, or find another way to explore the physical sensation of plunging part of your body into cold water.

As you do so, pray with any fears or promptings. Notice how the longer you stay in cold water, the more you get acclimatised to it. Likewise, prayer can seem uncomfortable and alien until we 'keep moving' and exercising within our relationship with God. Sing or pray with words from the hymn 'Father, hear the prayer we offer' to help you embrace risk in trusting God.

> *Father, hear the prayer we offer:*
> *not for ease that prayer shall be,*
> *but for strength that we may ever*
> *live our lives courageously.*
>
> Maria Willis (1824–1908)

# Grounded in worship

## Reflective/Intercession

Read Psalm 121.

Writing to a prayer group, Evelyn Underhill stressed that each person's worship 'will be different because what God wants from each of us is different'. Continuing with typical light-hearted, homely imagery, she wrote: 'all that we do must be grounded in worship. First, lift up our eyes to the hills, then turn to our own potato field and lightly fork in the manure.'

Her last major book, *Worship* (1936), looked at the diverse expression with which all main denominations honour Christ.

The double orientation to the natural and the supernatural, testifying at once to the unspeakable otherness of God transcendent and the intimate nearness of God incarnate, is felt in all the various expressions of genuine Christian worship. The monk or nun rising to recite the Night office that the Church's praise of God may never cease, the Quaker waiting in silent assurance on the Spirit given at Pentecost… the Catholic burning a candle before the symbolic image of the Sacred Heart… the Methodist or Lutheran pouring out his devotion in hymns to the Name of Jesus: the Orthodox bowed down in speechless adoration, the culminating moment of the Divine Mysteries, and the Salvationist marching to drum and tambourine behind the banner of the Cross—all these are here at one. Their worship is conditioned by a concrete fact; the stooping down of the Absolute to disclose himself within the natural human radius, the historical incarnation of the Eternal Logos within time.

Consider your own experience of worship, past and present. Has your experience or 'taste' in worship changed? What might account for any changes or abiding experiences? What might need challenging?

Conclude your time by praying for all denominations, asking for unity while honouring diverse expression within Christ's body.

## The House of the Soul

### Creative

After Evelyn Underhill's first visit to the House of Prayer at Pleshey, she commented exuberantly, 'The whole house seems soaked in love and prayer.' Promoted by retreat leaders like her, Pleshey became a spiritual home to many lay people seeking to build up their faithful commitment to Christ.

Do you have a special place—a church, building, maybe a favourite landscape—which seems 'soaked in love and prayer'? If you can, go to it or imagine the place. Ask that, by the Spirit's power, your prayers lovingly soak that place, and the people who visit it.

Underhill's *The House of the Soul* explores the idea of the soul being 'a two-storey house'. Above, she calls Faith, Hope and Charity 'the three supernatural virtues nourishing our life towards God, and having no meaning apart from God.' Her ground floor is sustained by the 'natural' virtues of Prudence, Temperance and Fortitude. Reflect on this lively portrait of our soul's downstairs area:

Most of us have inherited some ugly bits of furniture and unfortunate family portraits which we can't get rid of… nevertheless the soul does not grow strong merely by enjoying its upstairs privileges and ignoring its downstairs disadvantages, problems and responsibilities but only by tackling its real task of total transformation.

With these ideas in mind, spend time imagining your inner spiritual 'house'. Draw a simple two-storey building, then create separate rooms that speak of your innermost being. For example, you might have a living room full of things collected over the years; perhaps anything that regularly deflects your mind or emotions away from Jesus. Do you sense these once-precious objects crowd out space where you could spend relaxed time with him?

When you've sketched your soul's house, why not invite Jesus into each room? Perhaps you'll find yourself proudly opening certain doors to him, while others might have a 'keep out' sign! Whatever your instinctive feelings, avoid judging yourself. Simply write or draw your inner reactions and share them with Jesus.

# The triumph of prayer

## Intercession

Read Matthew 6:6–13.

> In the triumph of prayer
> Twofold is the spell.
> With the folding of hands
> There's a spreading of wings
> And the soul's lifted up to invisible lands
> And ineffable peace. Yet it knows, being there
> That it's close to the heart of all pitiful things;

*And it loses and finds, and it gives and demands;*
*For its life is divine, it must love, it must share*
*In the triumph of prayer.*

From *Theophanies* by Evelyn Underhill (1916)

In Matthew's Gospel, Christ teaches his disciples not only how to pray, but firstly what to do before they pray. At the beginning of each retreat, Evelyn Underhill would spell this out:

Shut the door. It is an extraordinarily difficult thing to do. Nearly everyone pulls it to and leaves it slightly ajar so that a whistling draught comes in from the outer world, with reminders of all the worries, interests, conflicts, joys and sorrows of daily life. But Christ said 'Shut', and he meant 'Shut'.

For Evelyn Underhill, prayer was adoration; any prayer focusing on personal issues could end up being 'mere devotionalism', akin to daydreaming. Instead, she recommended first considering the pattern of Christ's life. Then, using his prayer, likewise offer oneself to God's service.

Slowly pray through the Lord's Prayer. Stop after each line, savouring its flavour. Von Hügel compares this to letting a lozenge melt imperceptibly in your mouth. Aim to focus on intercession for others: family, friends, the Church and the world, rather than on your own wants and issues.

Next, take Underhill's image of prayer and belief fitting like 'hand in glove… the inside and outside of one single correspondence with God'. Find a glove and put it on your hand. Now pray about how prayer and action work together in your life. Is there a 'good fit'? Is your inner prayer life protected from intrusion, even in the busiest times? If you struggle to focus on worship and self-offering during your prayer time, aim to make this a habitual practice.

# Retreats

## Meditative

Until Evelyn Underhill, female retreat leaders were unknown. Lucy Menzies, a friend of Evelyn's and warden at Pleshey, writes in her memoir, 'There was never anything formal or stereotyped about her or the Retreats she gave. They were full of life, of zest, of humour.' Though she wore long lace caps when leading retreats, Underhill avoided intellectual approaches to God, instead suggesting meditation on Christ's ordinary activities during his earthly life: his incarnation, humble birth, growing up, experiencing friendship with his disciples and so forth.

Before any retreat at Pleshey, Underhill pinned material on the chapel door, including Henri de Tourville's advice on retreats:

> Make it with great simplicity... faults, weaknesses as you
> see in yourself, are not to cause you fear and anxiety, but
> rather humility and confidence... All that is consoling and
> encouraging... accept without reserve, remembering the
> unspeakable generosity of God who delights to overwhelm
> even the sinful and evil with gifts, especially when it lifts up its
> hands towards Him.

Today, hold your own mini retreat. Use Underhill's material from her retreat, *The end for which we were made*, in which she suggests selecting one or two Bible passages, including one scene from Christ's life.

> One of those times when He was able to withdraw from the
> bustling crowds... the compassionate service which filled
> His life... Consider what it would have been like to have
> been a Disciple, seeing and helping in that ministry, and,

because you had been taught to love, feeling as though you were shirking your task, not doing all you could. In that very situation, Christ said to you, 'Drop all this. Come apart,' and carried you away from… all the opportunities of practical Christianity to attend only to God…

Aware that any retreat might become a time of daydreaming or self-condemnation, Evelyn warns,

We come, in prayer, to open ourselves to the beauty and mystery of God brought to us in Christ—to learn more, to surrender more, to adore—not to scrape and sandpaper ourselves. When we have been quiet in the Great Presence for a while, we shall feel quite small and humble. It is far more important to feel small, humble and happy—as children do— than scraped or raw. Christ never makes people feel raw. Our own inverted egoism and wounded vanity do that.

When praying with a scene from Christ's life, she instructs,

Place yourself in God's presence. Consider that He says these words to you. Enter the picture which the words paint, and humbly kneel within it. There let His overshadowing love teach you. The Spirit of Christ speaks to you. Open your eyes and look at Him. Open your ears and hear what He says. (We've heard what He says over and over again and missed the heart of it just as we hear great music and miss its heart.) Consider what is being said to your soul. When your soul is reproved, see what fresh doors open. Look at what is put before you. Think it out before God… then turn your thoughts and deductions into prayer. Finally, resolve to act on the light you have received.

# Caring for souls

## Creative

> *But the fruit of the Spirit is love, joy, peace, longsuffering,*
> *gentleness, goodness, faith, meekness, temperance: against*
> *such there is no law.*
> GALATIANS 5:22–23 KJV

Some Christians are wary of having a Spiritual Director or 'soul friend', feeling no need for an intermediary between themselves and Jesus. Evelyn Underhill's Catholic orientation made her keen to avail herself of this sacrament, especially after the Great War when struggling to find a home in the Church.

In 1920, she gained at least one 'soul friend' on discovering the Spiritual Entente, a secret fellowship founded by an Italian Franciscan nun, Sorella Maria of Campello. The Entente encouraged prayer among ecumenical members who lived in ways that hopefully convinced others that Christ was present in all their respective churches. With friends such as Amy Turton, who made her aware of the Spiritual Entente, Underhill settled as an Anglican, becoming a Spiritual Director before running retreats at Pleshey.

Interestingly, while her green and flowered notebooks contain many self-critical reports of her own spiritual progress, Underhill's letters containing her direction for friends attack any morbid introspection. Instead they're full of common sense and warm humour. She writes that the fruits of the spirit are 'good subjects for meditation. A good gardener always has an idea of what he is trying to grow; without vision, even a cabbage patch will perish.'

I particularly enjoy her take on 'longsuffering' when writing to a friend in 1909:

As to the last crime on your list… 'dislike of pain', you need not take a very desponding view. My dear child, everyone dislikes pain, really—except a few victims of religious and other forms of hysteria. Even the martyrs, it has been said, had 'less joy of their triumph because of the pain they endured'. They did not want the lions; but they knew how to 'endure the cross' when it came. Do not worry your head about such things as this: but trust God and live your life bit by bit as it comes.

Keeping Underhill's encouragement in mind, take a large sheet of paper and create a personal chart. In one column, list each spiritual fruit. Add another, wider, column showing how and where you particularly 'outwork' their qualities. In a third column, jot down how you might work on weaknesses and build on any strengths, either with a spiritual friend, confessor or alone with Jesus. Refer back to this list often, praying for ways to share and practically develop this fruit.

# Time and eternity

## Meditative

Hanging in the House of Prayer's library, an embroidery belonging to Evelyn Underhill spells out one word—ETERNITY.

For a Christian to appreciate their destiny in eternity, Underhill paradoxically thought it vital to get a grip on 'time' and worldly commitments—explored in her essay, *The Mastery of Time*. Quoting Isaiah 28:16, 'He that believeth shall not make haste', she insisted that people who trust God do not get rattled.

A glance at Underhill's commitments shows it was vital that she mastered time. Her daytimes were generally spent studying or writing. She corresponded with friends or spiritual students in the evenings. Twice a week, she visited people living in the slums. Her rule of life included daily periods of prayer and devotional reading. She attended church twice a week. Childless, she kept watch over her parents, had a very active social life and enjoyed hobbies such as bookbinding, sailing and motoring.

Think about your own use of time, both 'working' and following the spiritual life. Are you balancing time doing both? Have you considered making a rule of life to help you balance activity and stillness?

Take the present situation as it is and try to deal with what it brings you, in a spirit of generosity and love. God is as much in the difficult home problems as in the times of quiet and prayer... Try especially to do His will there, deliberately seek opportunities for kindness, sympathy, and patience.

From *The Letters of Evelyn Underhill* (1947)

I remember once in the Alps finding myself alone in a high pasture surrounded by the strange, almost unearthly mountain life. I was filled then with that absolute contentment and solemn happiness... Above me I could only see the next bit of rough path, but on the other side of the valley I gazed at a great majestic range of snowy peaks and knew they were... waiting for me if only I would slog on, take a few more risks... I stood there, getting smaller and smaller and happier and happier as I realised my own place in that great world of beauty and wonder.

From *Light of Christ* by Evelyn Underhill (1932)

# Heaven a dance

## Poetry/Creative

> *Heaven's not a place…*
> *No! 'tis a dance*
> *Where love perpetual*
> *Rhythmical,*
> *Musical,*
> *Taketh advance*
> *Loved one to lover*
>
> From *Theophanies* by Evelyn Underhill (1916)

Today, either consider the above poem, or consider your personal 'glimpse of heaven' in the light of this quote from the broadcast talk *The Spiritual Life*:

> Has it never happened to you to lose yourself for a moment in a swift and satisfying experience for which you found no name? When the world took on a strangeness, and you rushed out to meet it, in a mood at once exultant and ashamed?… Those were onsets of involuntary contemplation; sudden partings of the conceptual veil. Dare you call them the least significant moments of your life?

Now creatively express in words, painting, dance or collage what the 'dance of heaven' could mean for you. Offer your 'dance' to God.

# God's peace

## Reflective

*And the peace of God, which passeth all understanding, shall keep your hearts and minds through Christ Jesus.*

PHILIPPIANS 4:7

Three aspects of Evelyn Underhill's life and teaching can particularly speak out today. Firstly, she knew the practical importance of the spiritual life for herself and every believer. Secondly, that life was for women and men, and was not just a private activity. Finally, she understood how the institutional Church could be off-putting to new believers, yet, by persevering, came to a joyful outward commitment to a specific church within the Christian family, writing: 'when we think of pews and hassocks... we tend to rebel... it seems far too stiff and institutional... Yet there it is; the Christian sequence is God—Christ—Spirit—Church—Eternal Life.'

With her life nearing its end, Underhill declared herself a pacifist, an unpopular stance at the outbreak of World War II. She had already embraced risks in serving others tirelessly when she could have sat back and lived a domestic existence of upper middle-class privilege. Instead, she kept in touch with people from all walks of life who wanted her advice and support, even when her health prevented her from leading retreats and retaining an active life. For many, her life showed God's transformative work offering peace on a much larger, all-encompassing level than any worldly attempts.

What does the peace of God mean to you—in the past, now and in anticipation of the future? Have you found parts of Underhill's legacy that resonate with or differ from your own experience of faith and worship? Try staying with these, praying for God's message to sink deeper and bring you peace. If there are struggles, why not sing words from the hymn 'Peace, perfect peace'?

# Choices

*Lynne Chitty*

## Wordswithoutspacesarehardtounderstand

### Introduction

What words are on our lips as we begin Advent? What jumble of words are crying out to be separated, sorted or silenced? How can we use this season to carve out space to make some good choices? Choosing is something most of us do every day. What to eat, what to wear, what to say, how to spend our time and resources. More careful or more daring consideration of our choices might perhaps be something we can use Advent to reflect on. Are the words we choose to use to define ourselves and others the right ones? Are they unkind? Untrue? Limiting?

Words matter. We are judged by our words. What we say or write helps others form their opinion of us. Through social media, our words can reach the other side of the world in a fraction of a second. Words are powerful; they can build up and they can destroy. First and last words are especially precious and particularly remembered. Most parents remember proudly the first words of their children. If we have sat at a bedside and heard someone's dying words, we are unlikely ever to forget them. We take notice of the first words of Presidents or Prime Ministers and are inspired by the last words of those who face death bravely and honestly.

The Bible is the Christian book of words. But whilst we have Jesus' last words from the cross recorded in the Gospels, only Mary and Joseph were privileged to hear his first spoken words as a child. We do have his first recorded words at the beginning of his ministry. In John, they are 'Come and see' (John 1:39 NRSV); in Mark, they are 'The time is fulfilled and the Kingdom of God has come near' (Mark 1:15).

As we start Advent, we will reflect on a single word each day and build a collage of these words. Use the suggestions given or collect and draw things to represent the word, or you may want to write or draw the word as appropriate for the journey the word has taken you on.

Choosing how to represent each word can be fun, so be daring, imaginative and creative.

*God of our Advent journey, may we hear your still small voice in our silence. May we embrace a fresh relationship with your Son, the Word made flesh, and be open to your Spirit as we reflect on the living words of scripture.*
*Amen*

Start your collage today with the word 'Advent'. Choose what materials you will use: cardboard, paper, fabric, etc. Choose something that reflects how you feel as Advent begins. You could colour or draw the word each day or make it out of string or wool or wrapping paper. Play with the word as much as you can.

# Repent

## Reflective

Read Mark 1:1–5.

Not a very fashionable word to begin with and certainly not a comfortable one. But it is where John the Baptist starts as he bursts on the scene in Advent and it is where we can start to be enriched by the opportunity Advent offers us. I wonder, though, if we can think of repentance in terms of change and choice—much more accessible and manageable words, but ones that don't let us off the hook or diminish the power or the challenge of what is at the heart of repentance, which is to turn back. To turn around and look at God, at ourselves, at our lives, at one another, at our world. To turn back from a journey that has taken us off track.

This Advent, what might you choose to change? A habit? An attitude? An injustice? A routine? Or could you change one room around and make a place where you can sit quietly and ask God to change you day by day? Like any journey, it is one step at a time. So be gentle with yourself as well as honest. Repentance isn't about beating yourself up, but about receiving God's grace.

*God of stability and change, may this Advent be a time of turning away from all that separates me from you and a turning towards your Son. Not despairing that I forever fall short but rejoicing that, through the gift of repentance, you have blessed me with the assurance of reconciliation, forgiveness and healing.*
*Amen*

Spend time creating the word 'Repent' and add it to your collage.

# Restore

### Creative

Read John 1:1–5 and verse 14.

John's prologue contains some of the most beautiful, intimate and poetic words in scripture. But what do they mean today as we come to Advent and prepare for another Christmas? How can we use these days to be drawn deeper into a relationship with God who is both mystery and yet, in Jesus, becomes flesh and blood?

The whole prologue is centred on the *Logos*—the word. In the Greek, *Logos* means more than just the spoken word. It refers also to the idea and thought behind the word, the vision, the plan, the wisdom that inspires it.

Perhaps paradoxically, it is in silence that we need to begin. The deep silence of our heart, the piercing silence of the world's sorrow, the resounding silence of emptiness, the fertile silence of prayer. It is silence that teaches us to listen and only then can we hear the Word made flesh calling to us.

In the silence, the poetry of John 1 speaks through the movement of the words, of communion. It finds fulfilment as the Word becomes flesh—to lead us into a new communion with God, a new relationship. We become one with God and receive the very life of God within us. Restorative love; God choosing to send his Son to restore a relationship disfigured by sin.

Is there something in your house you could restore through mending, polishing or cleaning? As you do this, allow God to restore you to his communion.

Draw or paint the word 'Restore'. What colours will you use? Add it to your collage.

# Respond

## Imaginative

Read Luke 1:26–38.

Imagine the scene: there you are, quietly getting on with life when an angel appears with a crazy message about you bearing God's son. You are a young woman, have had no relations with a man and yet you find yourself responding with 'Yes'.

Notice the emotions that are part of the journey to 'Yes'. With God, all things are possible.

Mary's response, and the words of her subsequent song 'Magnificat' when she visits her kinswoman Elizabeth, are still sung by choirs in cathedrals and churches every day at Evensong.

They have been and continue to be set to music beautifully and evocatively. The visit of the angel to Mary has been painted hundreds of times. A truly amazing encounter and an even more amazing response. Mary's response is a marker by which we can test our own response to a calling, or a challenge or a daily task. Every day we have situations and people to respond to in our families and lives and in the worldwide community. We are invited, too, to offer a response to God's love for us. Gratitude, thankfulness, awe, bewilderment, disbelief: all responses we may feel at one time or another. Maybe a little seed of an idea has been tucked away for a while but now might be the time to bring it to birth. Maybe a time set aside to hold a certain area of the world in prayer. Maybe even, and this perhaps the hardest of all, a response of 'No' if we are asked to do more than we know we can manage.

Add the word 'Respond' to your collage. Fill the letters with some of the responses you are making to God at the moment. Offer him your response as you create.

# Respect

### Creative

Read Matthew 1:18–25.

Even before the angel appeared to him in a dream, Joseph was going to act with respect, dignity and compassion. He would quietly annul the engagement and protect Mary from condemnation and possible punishment. After the dream he does what many would think unthinkable: he believes the angel, trusts that Mary hasn't been unfaithful and marries her. This is another response born of a deep faith in the God of the impossible and the unprecedented. We don't know if Joseph would have been respected for his decision. Was there gossip at the timing of Jesus' birth, were eyebrows raised? We don't know and perhaps we don't need to know. We can reflect on the integrity and the character of the man we glimpse briefly at Christmas and who then gently slips away.

*Father God, we give you thanks for Joseph, whom we barely know but who, with Mary, bore the astonishing events of Christ's birth in obedience and with a generous heart. When our lives are overturned by the unexpected, or you reach out to us in dreams, grant us the love and courage of Joseph, that we may be open to your prompting and fulfil your purposes for our lives.*
*Amen*

To add 'Respect' to your collage, look for a font on your computer that reflects the respect of Joseph for Mary. Print the word in your chosen font and add it to your collage.

# Relax

### Creative

As my Advent treat I am doing a 1000-piece jigsaw, hindered by my cat Eliza who insists on curling up in the box and takes great exception when I try to extract a new piece! The disappointment comes when you find that, after all your efforts, there are only 999 pieces, leaving a 'hole' in your magnificent picture, thus robbing you of any sense of satisfaction or achievement. Eventually having searched high and low, you just have to accept that it's missing. Either someone else has 1001 pieces, or it's in the hoover or, worse, in the cat!

Prayer can be a bit like that—a chance to lay out all the different colours and shapes of our life and to allow the Holy Spirit to work with us, making us more fully the beautiful picture that we are in God. Amidst that, there is the seemingly endless task of finding all the outside pieces, then the excitement of allowing the colours and features to draw us into their depths. Only then does the picture start to take real shape. Of course, we do the easy bits first and then grumble when we are left with all the sea and sky bits that look exactly the same. We want to give up because it's no fun anymore. Then there's the piece we can't find, just when we were beginning to feel rather pleased with our efforts.

Perhaps if Advent has become cluttered, or is tinged with a sense of 'if I had more time I'd be more holy', then have a go at a jigsaw, offering the time you spend on it to God and receiving it back as gift. Allow your 'jigsaw time' to be your special time. Enjoy feeling the pieces, enjoy seeing the picture take shape. Enjoy who you are amidst all your restlessness and inability to pray articulately, and your groping at trying to feel God's presence. Amidst all the complexities of our lives, we need a 'jigsaw time'; we need to relax a little.

*Gracious God, as I journey through Advent and get discouraged about my lack of progress, my lack of holiness, grant me the grace to relax and to embrace simple playfulness. May I be blessed with 'jigsaw times' and, piece by piece, become more fully your child, knowing that in you all is complete.*
*Amen*

Cut out the letters to make the word 'Relax' and then cut them into pieces and make a jigsaw of the letters for your collage.

# Prepare

## Prayer

Preparing is one of the great themes of Advent, and looking and listening are two of the most precious aspects we have been given as our journey unfolds. Whether it is looking at the vivid stars in a sky so dark it is ablaze, or listening to raindrops dripping on the roof, the sights and sounds from my cabin are God's gift to me. They are a way of receiving more of God as I become entwined with creation, her times and seasons, colours and decay, struggle and all her joy. We can choose to rush or to be still and allow all our senses to be immersed into the eternal treasure, held like a pearl in every passing moment.

Pray that as you look and listen day by day, drawing closer to Bethlehem and preparing for the birth of Christ, you may both see the sights and hear the sounds around you, but also the sights and sounds of the outcasts, the suffering, the abused. If we're not listening, we can settle in the inn of complacency and miss the cry of the stable. The cry of life newborn and the eternal, of Emmanuel, God with us and of Christmas, every moment, every day.

Write the word 'Prepare' and surround it with images of precious things you have encountered today. Add it to your collage.

# Presence

## Poetry

We can't always choose who is present with us in life—at home, at church, at work, on the bus. We have spells when we are more solitary and spells in which we are constantly surrounded by others. Some cause us to shout with joy and others, well, let's just say they are a bit more challenging! Advent and Christmas are the celebration of God's presence with us, in our world and in our hearts. The Christ child in all his vulnerability is a symbol of the God whose loving presence is both fragile and eternally strong. God chose and continues to choose to be present with us day by day.

Take a moment to be still today. Allow yourself to be drawn into the silence and to encounter the otherness and the presence of the love of God that dwells in the heart of silence.

*The silence of your love embraces me*
*I sense a smile*
*so still we sit, so still*
*Each breath is wonder*
*each thought is joy.*
*Unmarred by words*
*Unspoilt.*
*O perfect love*
*Explode.*
*Drench us, drown us*
*deafen us to all our self-made noise*
*To all except*
*the silence of your love*

Add the word 'Presence' to your collage. How will you respond to God's presence in the silence?

# Perspective

## Intercession

It's very easy to put ourselves in the centre of the universe and get everything out of perspective. We feel that our needs are more important, more urgent and we have every right to complain when things don't go our way.

We are at the centre of God's universe, all of us are—but together, not individually. God cares for each one of us and all of us. In the same way, we are called to care for one another, not to climb over one another on our way to what we feel we are owed or deserve. The truth is, we don't get what we deserve. Instead we get the love of God none of us deserve but all can embrace. It can change our lives and give us a passion for those on the margins whose voices aren't heard, whose needs aren't met. Some of them make life and death choices: to stay in a war zone or to flee; to risk the lives of their families on overcrowded boats or risk a long slow death in their homeland; to risk speaking out against an oppressive government or to watch in silence as others are imprisoned or killed.

At a time when, for some of us, the trickiest choice we have to make is what to buy for our friends or what to wear to the Christmas meal, add the word 'Perspective' to your collage with stories or headlines from newspapers or magazines that put your life's choices in perspective. Remember those who today have heart-wrenching choices to make for themselves or their families. If you are faced with a difficult choice yourself, add something to your collage that represents the decision to be made.

# Pain

## Reflective

It is easy to gloss over pain and not mention the heartache that Advent and Christmas bring to many.

At Christmas Jesus comes into our world through the blood, pain and vulnerability of a baby born in a stable to Mary and Joseph, who were entrusted with his nurture, upbringing, even his very life.

Some who are reading this may be pregnant themselves, or know someone who is. They have a date fixed in their mind, the date the baby is due; they are waiting, preparing with a mixture of excitement, anticipation and perhaps fear that they won't be up to the task of parenting.

For others, single or married, the birth of a child, the gift of motherhood or fatherhood will never be theirs. Looking through the Bible isn't always a comfort, not only because the word 'barren' is such a brutal one, but also because it crudely implies infertile women are cursed by God. It was a great stigma for a woman to be barren. The other difficulty about barren women in the Bible is that some famous examples offer heartfelt prayers and suddenly God answers them and grants them the gift of a child (whatever their age). God blesses them, restores them to full womanhood and their dreams come true. But for many today, their dreams don't come true, prayers aren't answered with the gift of a child and they, and their husbands or partners, bear inside them a pain that isn't easily talked about.

So what can the birth of Jesus at Christmas say to those carrying the inner grief of barrenness? Where is the joy they are supposed to feel?

In Jesus, God gives us all a son, his Son, born through Mary at Christmas as a gift for a world that was in turmoil then, as it is in turmoil now. A world turned in on itself, separated from its Creator spiritually, environmentally and in all its relationships. In Jesus we are invited to become one with God, to receive Jesus and to know, through him, that we ourselves are God's children. We are all part of that most wonderful moment when Mary gives birth to her son— God's Son, our Son and our redeemer.

So as we prepare for Christmas, whatever our circumstances, as we see pictures of a baby in a manger, and sing carols and reflect on the meaning of Christmas, perhaps we can ask the questions, 'What can I give birth to this Christmas in partnership with God?' or, 'What gift is God bestowing on me amidst all my hopes and fears?'

Jesus, the 'Word made flesh', comes that we might have life, and life in all its fullness. If Christmas is about anything, it is about new life: fragile, vulnerable, but ultimately eternal. We are drawn into and are a part of the great song of creation. We have something precious within us that God is calling us to bring to birth.

Add 'Pain' to your collage—not a comfortable word, but it is in our lives. Acknowledging that is important. Add the names of those individuals or groups who may find Christmas a painful time of year.

# Peace

## Poetry

Ann Lewin's poem 'Wachet auf' expresses the tension between the now of Advent and the rapidly approaching Christmas. It is a difficult choice to turn away from all that is expected of us. Choosing to say 'No' to the noise and hustle and bustle of this exciting but subtly corruptive time of year might be the best present you can give yourself and others.

Advent.
Season when
Dual citizenship
Holds us in
Awkward tension.

The world, intent on
Spending Christmas,
Eats and drinks its way to
Oblivion after dinner.
The Kingdom sounds
Insistent warnings:
Repent, be ready,
Keep awake.
He comes.

Like some great fugue
The themes entwine:
The Christmas carols,
Demanding our attention
In shops and pubs,
Bore their insistent way

*Through noise of traffic;*
*Underneath, almost unheard,*
*The steady solemn theme of*
*Advent.*

*With growing complexity,*
*Clashing, blending,*
*Rivals for our attention,*
*Themes mingle and separate,*
*Pulling us with increasing*
*Urgency,*
*Until in final resolution,*
*The end attained,*
*Harmony rests in aweful*
*Stillness, and*
*The child is born.*

*He comes,*
*Both Child and Judge.*

*And will he find us*
*Watching?*

*May I find peace enough this Advent to still the anxiety of my life, beauty enough to colour my routine, music enough to enrich my silence, courage enough to overcome my hesitancy, grace enough to minister to my disappointments and love enough to bear all things, to cherish all things and to carry all things in prayer.*
*Amen*

Make the word 'Peace' on your collage bigger than all the other words. Make it bright so that it really stands out. You could use some of the tinsel, shiny paper and glitter around at this time.

# Perseverance

## Spotlight/Going out

Etty Hillesum, a young Jewish woman, left a legacy of letters and diaries describing life in Amsterdam during German occupation. With her parents and brother Mischa, she was sent to Auschwitz in Poland, where she died on 30 November 1943, aged 29.

In spite of all the suffering she saw, she refused to hate. She was able to say, 'Despite everything, life is full of beauty and meaning' and above all she chose to go on. She wrote, 'There are moments when I feel like giving up or giving in—but I soon rally again and do my duty as I see it—to keep the spark of life inside me ablaze.'

Incredible words, which each one of us can reflect on in this, the darkest time of year, as we continue to make our way to the stable at Bethlehem where in the darkest time of night a star lit up the sky and angels sang a song of glory.

As you add the word 'Perseverance' to your collage, make it blaze out. If you can see the stars where you live, look up at them in the dark sky and remember Etty and all those whose courage and love of life continue to be an inspiration. Go back to the prologue of John's Gospel (v. 1:5): 'The light shines in the darkness and the darkness did not overcome it.'

# O come, O come, Emmanuel

*Sally Smith*

## O come, O come, Emmanuel

### Introduction/Creative

The words of the well-loved Advent carol, 'O come, O come, Emmanuel', come originally from a twelfth-century Latin hymn that was translated into English in 1851 by John Mason Neale (1818–66). The words are based on five of the Advent 'O Antiphons' which were used at the service of Vespers in the days immediately preceding Christmas. The tune usually used for this hymn (*Veni Emmanuel*) has its origins in 15th-century France.

The words transport us back to the time of the Old Testament to remember the God of David and the desert, but also move us forward to the coming of the Son of God, the rejoicing of God with us, and remind us why this happened. They then point into the future towards the rejoicing that will be at the second coming. There is a strong theme of the release of the people from Satan's hold over humanity through the coming of Christ, reminding us of how this took place and that it still needs to happen today. The music and the words capture the longing and hoping for what is still to come and we join in with the yearning for the 'not-yet'. It can mirror that excitement and sorrow that often accompany this run-up to Christmas. It also contains many of the different titles given to the coming Messiah in the Bible that we hear so often at this time of year.

Slowly read through the words of the hymn. As you read, notice which words catch your attention. Pause by those words, look at them and accept them before moving on. You could collect the words that have struck you as you read and put them into a word diagram, either drawing it by hand or using one of the many websites available that will do this for you. Keep your diagram by you as you head towards Christmas.

# Emmanuel shall come

### Reflective

> O come, O come, Emmanuel
> And ransom captive Israel
> That mourns in lonely exile here
> Until the Son of God appear
> Rejoice! Rejoice! Emmanuel
> Shall come to thee, O Israel.

The first verse calls for Emmanuel, 'God with us', to pay the ransom for Israel, to set the people free from their captors. Israel is in exile, waiting for the coming of the Son of God who will rescue them and release them.

In Isaiah 7:14 is the prophecy that God will come and be with his people in the form of a child born to a young woman. This is a cry for both the children of Israel seeking release and for us seeking the coming of God again. But they, and we, are called to rejoice, for God is coming and he will be with us.

If you have a nativity set, take the empty manger, or make a simple bed for a baby from a scrunched-up towel or blanket. Sit before the empty crib, waiting in anticipation for the coming birth.

Notice the emotions within you as you wait.

What is it you are waiting for? Is it Christ's birth at Christmas or are you looking beyond that to Christ coming again?

What might you need to do to get ready?

Talk to God the Father about your waiting and what is happening in the waiting.

Are you putting the case for hurrying things up, or do you want to prolong the waiting?

Listen to what God the Father finds in the waiting and where Christ is in it.

# Until the Son of God appear

### Intercession

The impending arrival of Emmanuel, God with us, is giving the children of Israel hope; they are looking beyond their current situation to the time which is to come when their God will again be with them.

Each day in the news, we read and hear of those who are living lives seemingly without hope. They may be people who are living in war-torn countries or under oppressive regimes. Or they may have escaped one situation to find there is no way forward in their new lives and they are as stuck as they were before. It could be those living in poverty, unable to find a way out and living day to day without the hope of improvement.

Sit with God before an unlit candle alongside those without hope. Pray that Emmanuel shall come to them. Light the candle as a symbol of that hope available for them, receiving with them the hope of the light of Christ coming into their world.

# The shoot of Jesse

## Going out

> *O come, Thou Rod of Jesse, free*
> *Thine own from Satan's tyranny*
> *From depths of Hell Thy people save*
> *And give them victory o'er the grave*
> *Rejoice! Rejoice! Emmanuel*
> *Shall come to thee, O Israel.*

> *A shoot shall come out from the stump of Jesse and a branch*
> *shall grow out of his roots.*
> ISAIAH 11:1 NRSV

> *On that day the root of Jesse shall stand as a signal to the*
> *peoples; the nations shall inquire of him and his dwelling shall*
> *be glorious.*
> ISAIAH 11:10

Jesse was the father of David, so the new growth referred to in these passages from Isaiah refers to a new beginning from the house of David. These are not the new shoots that come from a healthy tree, adding growth upon growth. These are the struggling shoots that come from a 'stump' of a tree, one that has died or been cut down and is close to dying; it produces new shoots as a final effort to ensure it continues to exist.

Similarly, the branches are not new branches growing from healthy existing branches; these are coming from the root stock, from the heart, the very essence of the tree. The words 'shall shoot' could be translated as 'bear fruit' or be given as 'shall sprout', giving an image of life bursting out from the old, seemingly lifeless, stump.

Go outside and see if you can find any stumps or old trees with new branches that have sprouted out from the roots. At this time of year, they may not look particularly full of life, but see how they are bringing new life to the tree. Notice how many shoots there are and where they are coming from.

Imagine what they will bring to the plant as spring arrives and how they will change the life and appearance of the tree.

What would the tree be like without this new life?

Are there other trees around that have not grown new shoots? Compare the two and how you respond to each.

Are there areas of your life, or that of the community in which you live and worship, that are like the old stump?

As you look at the sprouting stump, hold those areas before God and ask that they too may receive the new growth and life that comes from the roots and contain the same origins in new forms. Imagine that new life coming from the stripped tree. Ask God to sprout those new branches so that the new season can begin.

# House of David

## Imaginative

> *But you, O Bethlehem of Ephrathah, who are one of the little clans of Judah, from you shall come forth for me one who is to rule in Israel, whose origin is from of old, from ancient days.*
> MICAH 5:2

It is from Bethlehem that a ruler will emerge to shepherd God's people. Bethlehem is the family home of King David—David, the youngest of the brothers, the one we remember as standing before Goliath with just his sling and stones, the smallest and overlooked one.

I find that in the bottom of many bags, boxes or drawers there is often something small and seemingly insignificant that is forgotten and ignored. Look in your bag, or a box of buttons, or your cutlery or desk drawer, somewhere that small things can get lost in the dark corners, or beneath larger and more frequently used items. Dig deep and find that small item at the bottom, forgotten and left in the dark corners and the dust.

Hold this item and sit with it before God.

Imagine being that item. What did it feel like being left, deserted, in the dark? What was it like to be forgotten, to have your worth and usefulness ignored?

Relive with your item the experience of a few minutes ago when the light shone, you were uncovered and then picked out and held in a warm hand. Suddenly you were valued. Notice how it feels to be held and cherished after your time in the dark.

Feel the love of God as you hold your now loved item. Listen as God tells you of your value and worth to him and of his plans for your future growth and use.

You might want to keep your item for a while near where you pray, awarding it its true value and worth and being reminded of your own true value and worth before God.

# Thy people save

## Imaginative/Creative

We often glibly say that we have been saved by Jesus, that he died to save us, but what is it that he saved us from? To begin to explore what it is that we have been saved from, try imagining what your life would be like without Jesus. What might you be doing? Who might you be with? For some this will be easy, and will be a reminder of a past life that is over. For others this may be harder; after a life lived with God, it is difficult to imagine what life might have been like without that presence. Look at some of those in need in your locality, in your town or in the wider world. What can you learn from them of life without Jesus?

Cut some headlines and pictures from newspapers or print them from the internet. As you place them around a crib from a nativity set or a card depicting Jesus in the manger, acknowledge that it was for these people that Jesus left his heavenly Father and came to earth as a vulnerable little baby. Sit with them, holding them before the God who knows what it is to be exiled from family and country.

Add a picture or something to represent yourself, for he also came to save you. As you place this image, receive the gift of God giving his life to save you.

Spend time before Jesus and use the refrain of the carol, but end it with your name instead of 'Israel'.

> Rejoice! Rejoice! Emmanuel
> Shall come to thee, O Israel.

# Thou Day-Spring

**Reflective**

> *The people who walked in darkness have seen a great light; those who lived in a land of deep darkness—on them light has shined.*
>
> ISAIAH 9:2

> *Arise, shine; for your light has come, and the glory of the Lord has risen upon you. For darkness shall cover the earth, and thick darkness the people; but the Lord will arise upon you, and his glory will appear over you.*
>
> ISAIAH 60:1–2

> *O come, Thou Day-Spring, come and cheer*
> *Our spirits by Thine advent here*
> *Disperse the gloomy clouds of night*
> *And death's dark shadows put to flight*
> *Rejoice! Rejoice! Emmanuel*
> *Shall come to thee, O Israel.*

'Thou Day-Spring' could equally have been translated as 'O rising sun' or 'O morning star'. Whatever the words, it refers to that early morning light which creeps into the darkness of the night and slowly takes over. It gives us the joy of the morning after the dark shadows and hidden areas of the night. Isaiah mentions a 'great light', suggesting that this light appeared somewhat more quickly and surprisingly than we are used to.

At some times of the year and in some parts of the world, the sun does come suddenly in the morning, highlighting the sharp contrast between the dark and the light; at other times and in other places the sun takes its time to arrive, lingering as it lights up each corner individually and giving time to savour the changes and colours of the dawn.

The experience of switching on the light in the late afternoon, as the daylight begins to fade and we are struggling to continue to read, is very different from the experience of waking up in a dark room in the middle of the night and being blinded by the brightness as you switch on the light. The carol suggests both the cheering of light in the gloom and the blinding light as night's shadows are sent on their way.

Try to find a way to experience that sudden change from darkness into light. You could try sitting in a darkened room. Give your eyes plenty of time to get used to the dark. As you wait, notice the darkness and its effect on you. Seek the comfort of God in the darkness as you experience 'death's dark shadows'. The greater the experience of the dark, the greater will be the rejoicing over the light when it comes.

Suddenly switch on the brightest light in the room. Try and notice all that you see and feel in that moment as the light puts the shadows to flight. Experience God's great light in your comparatively small light.

Rejoice at the coming of the light into the world.

# Disperse the gloomy clouds

**Reflective**

In 1906, T.A. Lacey translated the third line of the Day-spring verse as, 'Dispel the long night's lingering gloom'.

Some days at this time of year seem to have a lingering gloom, and often a light will lift our spirits as well as aid our eyes. A flame can have a greater effect in giving a living light.

On one of those gloomy December days, light a candle and let it burn, giving a living light to your room. Spend some time watching the flame and allowing its light to pierce you.

Return to the light over the day (or days) ahead and remember the living light which does more than brighten a dark winter day.

# The key of the house of David

**Reflective/Intercession**

*I will place on his shoulder the key of the house of David; he shall open, and no one shall shut; he shall shut, and no one shall open.*

ISAIAH 22:22

> *O come, Thou Key of David, come*
> *And open wide our heavenly home*
> *Make safe the way that leads on high*
> *And close the path to misery*
> *Rejoice! Rejoice! Emmanuel*
> *Shall come to thee, O Israel.*

A key is a significant item with great power. It can open and it can close; it can keep in or let out. The holder of the key has power to allow and to refuse. In this sense, we are using the word 'key' to mean the metal item which locks or unlocks a door, but we also use the word for that important piece of knowledge or action that will enable us to solve a problem or find a way of making progress. The key to a whole organisation may be one person who has the power to allow progress or stop it. The key in a relationship may be one person whose attitudes can so influence the other that they are enabled or disabled by the keyholder's actions.

We can unlock and open wide the way for others to meet and follow Jesus, or keep the key safely hidden and deny them access. This can be through those with whom we don't share our faith, as well as those we fail to encourage in the growth of their faith.

Find a key you use regularly. As you hold it, think of the people you could unlock; the people you could encourage or have a conversation with that might make a difference to them. Put the key in its lock and slowly turn it. As you turn the mechanism, allow the people you are thinking of to be opened. As you see the difference the key makes, watch the difference this makes to those people. Ask God to help you to turn the key, open the door and keep it open.

When you next use your key, remember that opening and hold that person or people before God, asking that he continues to open them and keep the door open.

# God of Moses

## Reflective/Creative

*The Lord, the Lord, a God merciful and gracious, slow to anger, and abounding in steadfast love and faithfulness, keeping steadfast love for the thousandth generation, forgiving iniquity and transgression and sin…*

EXODUS 34:6–7A

> *O come, O come, Thou Lord of might*
> *Who to Thy tribes, on Sinai's height*
> *In ancient times didst give the Law*
> *In cloud, and majesty and awe*
> *Rejoice! Rejoice! Emmanuel*
> *Shall come to thee, O Israel.*

We are reminded in the final verse of the carol that it is the God of Moses whose presence with us we are to rejoice over. Moses met with God on Mount Sinai and was given the ten commandments, the laws by which the people were to live. Moses met with God in the cloud and the people were warned not to try and ascend the mountain to meet with God. They were to stay at the bottom and wait for Moses to return, for this was holy ground. When Moses descended the mountain with the second set of stone tablets with the ten commandments written on, his face was shining, such is the power and glory of God.

What ten 'rules' would challenge you to live a life worthy of a follower of God? These may be a modern reflection of the biblical ten commandments, or could be ten completely different laws.

As you think about what would impact on your life, write out your 'rules' and keep them somewhere where you can see them and be reminded of them. Do you feel able to follow these over the next week? Perhaps you could consider keeping them throughout next year (an early New Year's Resolution, maybe).

# In cloud and majesty and awe

## Prayer

> Then Moses went up on the mountain, and the cloud covered the mountain… Now the appearance of the glory of the Lord was like a devouring fire on the top of the mountain.
>
> EXODUS 24:15, 17

We read several times of Moses ascending Mount Sinai to meet with God in a cloud or amidst smoke. The mountain becomes holy ground and the people are forbidden to tread on it or to look at God. This is the God whom Moses looks at and his face shines from the experience when he returns to the base of the mountain.

Later, the shepherds are awed and terrified by the glory of the angels who bring the news of Jesus' birth. Traditionally we then picture them kneeling by the manger as they worship 'God with us'.

Kneel with Moses and with the shepherds before God in majesty and awe. If you have a nativity scene, place a kneeling shepherd by the manger and join him in homage before the baby.

Rejoice that God comes to us and is Emmanuel, God with us.

# O come, O come Emmanuel

## Poetry

Slowly reread the words of the carol, this time allowing the memories of the time you have spent with them to surface.

As you read the lyrics, notice which words catch your attention now and what happens inside as you pause over certain sections.

What has been the main message of the words for you? How would you sum them up in a few sentences? What of the carol do you carry forward towards Christmas?

As you hear or sing the carol, revisit those places where you have encountered God and allow the words to speak afresh to you over the Christmas season. Remember to rejoice, for God has come to us already and is Emmanuel, God with us.

*Dorinda Miller*

# The tree of your life

## Grown from seed

### Introduction

After all the planning and preparations, Christmas is here! May your day be (or have been) filled with peace and joy and love and laughter as you celebrate the birth of Jesus, Prince of Peace, with your family and friends!

As the year draws to a close, we will use the analogy of a tree to reflect on our lives.

In his first letter to the Corinthians Paul writes:

*When you put a seed into the ground, it doesn't grow into a plant unless it dies first. And what you put in the ground is not the plant that will grow, but only a bare seed of wheat or whatever you are planting. Then God gives it the new body he wants it to have. A different plant grows from each kind of seed.*

1 CORINTHIANS 15:36–38 NLT

The laws of nature seem, in many ways, to be in stark contrast to the pace of life in our day and age. We have the expectation of instant access to information and communication, and many people are caught up in a whirl of activities and responsibilities. Not so the seed, planted in the ground, growing silently, in solitude, out of sight, using the material within it to grow roots, until the seedling emerges above ground to gain its nutrients from the air, sunlight and water.

Like seeds we grew silently, in solitude, in the safety of our mother's wombs, as did Jesus. Even though he was with God in the beginning, he came as a baby and lived on earth, growing up in relative obscurity until he began his ministry.

*In the beginning was the Word, and the Word was with God, and the Word was God. He was with God in the beginning. Through him all things were made; without him nothing was made that has been made. In him was life, and that life was the light of all mankind. The light shines in the darkness, and the darkness has not overcome it.*

JOHN 1:1–5 NIV

# Create a tree

## Creative

Take a piece of paper or use a page in your journal and draw a tree— no artistic skill is necessary! It is simply to aid you in the reflections this week. The tree needs to have roots, trunk and branches. On the ground to the left of the tree, draw a large watering can, and on the ground to the right of the tree, draw a wheelbarrow with fruit in it. The drawing should not be too small, as you will be writing on parts of it over the course of the week.

The tree represents you and your life. Begin by considering the roots and writing down, on them or beside them, what they consist of for you, for example: faith, family, friends, finances, dreams, hopes, fears.

Now put your drawing to one side and read the following verse slowly, three times, and allow it to speak to you in the stillness.

> *Let your roots grow down into him, and let your lives be built on him. Then your faith will grow strong in the truth you were taught, and you will overflow with thankfulness.*
>
> COLOSSIANS 2:7 NLT

# Look at the trunk

## Creative

Today we move above ground to consider the trunk of the tree. The trunk is the core from which the branches grow and protrude and, together with the leaves, provide the tree's identity. As Thomas Merton wrote in *New Seeds of Contemplation*, 'The more a tree is like itself, the more it is like God.'

As you know, trees are always growing and changing with the seasons. In the late spring/early summer, many of them have shoots springing up from the base of their trunks or sprouting out of branches which have been cut back or broken. These shoots are diverting energy and growth away from more established parts of the tree. In the same way, we all have things on our hearts and minds that could distract us or hinder our time of reflection.

One way of overcoming this is through the following exercise:

Draw some shoots at the base of your tree's trunk. Then imagine that each shoot is something that is currently on your mind, that you need to let go of, so that it will not distract you during this time of quiet and reflection.

Either scribble over each one in turn or write a key word that sums up each concern beside it. When you have done so, be still for a few moments in God's presence.

Now turn your attention to the trunk. What condition is it in? Mature and strong? Vulnerable and weak? Storm damaged or weather beaten? Jot down the key words for you on or beside the trunk.

We can read the previous weather patterns in the rings of trees. These rings can show us the temperatures, storms and sunlight of different growing seasons. In a sense, the same is true of us. The seasons that we travel through shape and mould us, and the impact of storms and challenges serve to transform us into who we were created to be.

> Every moment and every event of every man's life on earth plants something in his soul.
>
> Thomas Merton, *New Seeds of Contemplation* (1972)

# Consider the branches

## Reflective

Today we move further up the tree to consider the branches. But before you do so, read John 15:1–2 and 4–6.

Bearing in mind these verses, consider the branches on your tree. Are they full of healthy new shoots and leaves? Are they bare and barren? Are they storm damaged and weather beaten? Is there any dead wood? Are there any missing branches and, if so, what are they? Has there been any pruning or is there a need for pruning? Jot down the key words and themes for you, on the branches of the tree you have drawn.

Finally, read the following verses from Jeremiah and be encouraged that, whatever the current state of our branches, we can have confidence and hope.

> *But blessed are those who trust in the Lord*
> *and have made the Lord their hope and confidence.*
> *They are like trees planted along a riverbank,*
> *with roots that reach deep into the water.*
> *Such trees are not bothered by the heat*

*or worried by long months of drought.*
*Their leaves stay green,*
*and they never stop producing fruit.*
JEREMIAH 17:7–8

# Count the fruit

## Reflective

Now we move on to consider the fruit of the tree. In your drawing at the beginning of the week, you placed a wheelbarrow at the base of the tree.

What is the fruit in your life? Is it in evidence? Is it growing and forming? Has it been harvested? Jot down the key words and themes for you at this time, on or around the wheelbarrow.

In the Gospels there are references to identifying and knowing a tree by its fruit. For example, in Matthew 12:33 we read:

*If you grow a healthy tree, you'll pick healthy fruit. If you grow a diseased tree, you'll pick worm-eaten fruit. The fruit tells you about the tree.*
THE MESSAGE

Paul picks up this theme in his letter to the Galatians when he speaks about the fruit of the spirit. Read Galatians 5:22–23.

Spend time with Paul's words and those that you wrote on your wheelbarrow, reflecting on how visible the fruit of the Spirit is in your life at the moment. From those Paul mentions, which ones do you want to cultivate in the coming year?

# Feed the tree

## Reflective

As the year draws to a close, it is a good time to look back at the past year and to look forward to the New Year. 'The Lord says, "I will teach you the way you should go; I will instruct and advise you"' (Psalm 32:8 GNT). Before you complete your reflection on the tree, by considering what promotes its growth and well-being, take a few moments to reflect on the past year and to recall the times that the Lord did indeed show you the way to go during it.

- How did he do this for you?
- Did you hear his voice and discern his will swiftly or did his guidance come more slowly over time?
- What did you learn from this process?
- How did it encourage you in your faith?

Now, in order for a tree to grow, it needs certain vital elements such as water and sun. If you have not already done so, draw a watering can at the bottom of the tree. Take a few moments to consider what are the life-giving and nourishing elements that you need for your life, in order to grow and mature and to maintain good health. Ask the Lord, 'What do I do to feed the tree with good things?' When you have done so, ask, 'Lord, what else would you like me to do, in order to strengthen my growth?' Write down the key words/themes for you on or around the watering can. Then reflect on:

- What type of season is your tree currently going through?
- What are the signs and symptoms of this season?
- What are God's promises for it?

### The Tree of Life
*What delight comes to those who follow God's ways!...*
*They will be standing firm like a flourishing tree*
*planted by God's design,*
*deeply rooted by the brooks of bliss;*
*bearing fruit in every season of their lives.*
*They are never dry, never fainting,*
*ever blessed, ever prosperous.*

PSALM 1:1A, 3 TPT

God's hand is over every part of your tree; commend it to him and pray for his blessing and protection to cover it, both now and throughout the coming year.

# As a Child

*Phil Steer*

## Discipline

> *Endure hardship as* discipline; *God is treating you as his
> children. For what children are not disciplined by their father?*
>
> HEBREWS 12:7, NIV 1984, emphasis mine

Some time ago, England was shocked by several days of rioting and
looting that broke out across London and elsewhere. In my home
town, on the outskirts of London, an 11-year-old boy was charged
with taking part in the looting of a department store.

In the inevitable debate and discussion that followed, there were
many different opinions about the social and economic causes of
the riots, and of the action that needed to be taken to deal with
the rioters and to prevent it happening again in the future. One
common cry, however, was the need for parents to provide greater
discipline for their children.

There is a well-known saying, 'Spare the rod and spoil the child'—
in other words, if you fail to discipline your child, then he will fail
to develop a good character and fail to grow into the person that
he could have become. In the Bible, the book of Proverbs contains
similar instruction: 'He who spares the rod hates his son, but he
who loves him is careful to discipline him' (Proverbs 13:24), and
'Do not withhold discipline from a child; if you punish him with the
rod, he will not die' (Proverbs 23:13). The idea is 'short term pain
for long term gain'.

It is arguable that, in the past, children suffered from too much
discipline, constrained and restrained in their natural childlike

exuberance, and subject to unnecessary and inappropriate levels of physical and emotional punishment from parents, teachers and even the law of the land. In recent years, however, it could be said that the pendulum has swung the other way. Our desire for our children to feel loved and valued, and our fear of them being abused, has arguably caused us to withhold discipline, or else so soften its blow that it ceases to be effective.

But if we find it hard to know how best to discipline our children and young people, then how much harder do we find it to know how it is that God disciplines us? Some see him as an austere father or strict headmaster or severe judge, and consider every hardship and misfortune as some form of discipline or punishment. Others know him to be a loving and merciful God, know that Jesus has taken the punishment for all our sin and wrong-doing and so never expect the Father's discipline and never recognise it when it comes.

It is neither right nor healthy to assume that all—or, indeed, most—of the hardships that we experience are the result of God disciplining us for some wrong-doing. On the other hand, we do not want to miss or ignore those times when he does discipline and correct us. As the writer of the book of Hebrews counsels, 'Do not make light of the Lord's discipline, and do not lose heart when he rebukes you, because the Lord disciplines those he loves, and he punishes everyone he accepts as a son' (Hebrews 12:5–6). We need somehow to find the right balance between these two extremes: between missing what is the Lord's discipline and agonising about what isn't.

Quite understandably, children feel very aggrieved if they are disciplined when they believe that they have done nothing wrong. Because of this, a good parent (or teacher) will never discipline a child without making it clear to him why they are doing so. If this is the case with imperfect human parents, then how much more so with our perfect heavenly Father? But let's be honest, most of us are usually only too well aware when we have 'sinned and fallen short of the glory of God' (Romans 3:23). Standing before him, we cannot help but feel like disobedient children before their parents. We may make excuses and try to shift the blame, but deep down we know when we are in the wrong. This being the case, if we genuinely struggle to identify why God might be disciplining us, and he appears to be staying resolutely silent on the subject, then it is unlikely that we should see our hardship as his discipline.

The writer of the book of Hebrews reminds us that 'our fathers disciplined us for *a little while* as they thought best' (Hebrews 12:10, italics mine); and Paul, writing to the church in Corinth, says to them, 'I see that my letter hurt you, but only for *a little while...*' (2 Corinthians 7:8, emphasis mine). To cause someone—and especially a child—to suffer for an extended period is not discipline, it's abuse; and it goes without saying that our heavenly Father is not an abusive parent. God will discipline us for a little while only; anything more—any hardship that drags on and on—is unlikely to be sent by him.

Of course, being disciplined is not a pleasant experience—and it isn't meant to be. But the pain is not the purpose of discipline—is not an end in itself. Rather, as the writer of Hebrews recognises, it is there to produce 'a harvest of righteousness and peace for those who have been trained by it' (Hebrews 12:11). Writing to the church in Corinth, Paul distinguishes between the 'godly sorrow' that results from the Father's discipline and the 'worldly sorrow' that has its roots elsewhere: 'Godly sorrow brings repentance that leads to salvation and leaves no regret, but worldly sorrow brings death' (2 Corinthians 7:10). If we feel condemned and lose heart, then we are not receiving God's discipline, for this will always have a positive outcome, and ultimately leave us feeling encouraged and uplifted. It is given to help us on our walk with him, not to hold us back and drag us down.

As parents, there are a number of ways in which we can discipline our children. We can 'tell them off', admonishing and reprimanding, speaking to them in strong words, raising our voice, perhaps even shouting. We can send them to their room or, with younger children, tell them to 'sit on the bottom stair'. We can withdraw a privilege or prevent them from doing something they want to do: watch the television, play on the computer, see a friend. Teenage children may be 'grounded', and not allowed to go out and 'do their own thing'. Though contentious, some parents may consider it appropriate to use limited physical pain and smack their children when they are naughty.

In all of these ways, God our heavenly Father can discipline us, his children. He can speak words of admonishment and rebuke: through the Bible, through the 'inner voice' of his Holy Spirit, and through the words of others. He can send us from his presence and from the companionship of others, compelling us to take some 'time out' on our own, and to consider our behaviour. He can step in and prevent us from doing something that we want to do, frustrating the plans we make for ourselves. And perhaps there are even times when some form of limited pain and suffering is the only way he can get through to us.

Now, I well appreciate how hard it can be to discern the Father's discipline in amongst the inevitable difficulties of everyday life. And I am aware also that some might see God's punishment in serious illness or other personal tragedy—which is not what I mean at all. I would simply suggest that, if things begin to go less well for us, if we feel that there has been a lessening of God's presence, of his blessing, of his hand upon our lives, then this may be his discipline. When such situations arise, therefore, we should not pass them off without a thought. Rather, we should have our eyes and ears and hearts and minds open to receive any correction that God might have for us, that we might be trained by it and brought to repentance. Remember, if it is of God, then we will know in our heart-of-hearts what it is we have done wrong, the discipline will last 'only for a little while' and, when acted upon, will leave us feeling better able to continue our journey of faith.

> *We have all had human fathers who disciplined us and we respected them for it. How much more should we submit to the Father of our spirits and live!*
>
> HEBREWS 12:9

# The House of Retreat, Pleshey

*Stewart McCredie*

When you arrive in Pleshey, it's hard to believe that you are just 35 minutes north-east of London. The peace and stillness in the village is such a contrast to that of the bustling city where so many are preoccupied with business and life. Arriving at the House of Retreat, there is a tangible peace and atmosphere that, some say, is like nothing experienced anywhere else. It has been said; 'Perhaps the prayer of so many years has soaked into its very walls; perhaps it is one of those "thin" places where heaven and earth come close.'

For over 600 years there has been a place of prayer within the serene village of Pleshey in the heart of Essex. In 1399, the then Duke of Gloucester chose Pleshey as the home for a new College of Augustinian Canons. 1906 saw the Anglican sisters of the congregation of the Servants of Christ visit the village. They were so impressed with the peace of the village that they bought the property where the house now stands. In 1909, the house was rebuilt as a convent and, since that time, has been maintained as a House of Prayer.

From 1912 the nuns advertised annual retreats and in 1914 the Diocese of Chelmsford rented the convent as a retreat house until 1927, when it purchased the property and the first Diocesan Retreat House came into being.

In those early years, Evelyn Underhill was most influential in the life of the House, not just spending time here on personal retreat herself, but also leading a number of retreats for others. It is largely due to Evelyn that the Retreat House became so popular.

In 1932, whilst leading a retreat at Pleshey entitled 'Light of Christ', Evelyn said something that is just as relevant today as it would appear to have been then:

> … taking the soul from its normal preoccupations and placing it in an atmosphere and condition in which, with the minimum of distraction, it can attend to and realise God. And this in essence is a retreat.

In the same retreat, Evelyn commented:

> Isn't it worthwhile to make some effort to create and keep going houses in which so great a thing can be done? Our increased capitulation to pace and noise makes it more and more necessary to provide such opportunities for realising our spiritual status, and learning the width of the chasm which separates deep from distracted prayer. It is not easy under everyday conditions to learn and maintain the art of steadfast attention to God.

The house is experiencing ever-increasing numbers of individuals taking that time out to minimise the distraction Evelyn described—even switching off their tablets and mobile phones!

Since those early days of the 20th century, the House has continued to develop and provide retreats for individuals and groups from all walks of life and experience. As a result of generous legacies and donations from groups and individuals, significant improvements have been made to the house and associated buildings. Of the 27 bedrooms, 17 are now en suite; a lift from the ground to the first floor now provides access for those with mobility issues; and the ground floor access and facilities have been greatly improved for wheelchair users. We also offer self-catering facilities, namely the 16th-century Gatehouse and Parsonage Cottage.

A familiar quote of Evelyn's, that we use regularly when talking about the House or the benefit of making a retreat, is from her book *Mysticism*:

For a lack of attention a thousand forms of loveliness elude us every day.

How true that is for so many of us, whether it is God's creation, those we meet through life, or the daily realisation of God's love for each one of us.

Be encouraged, whether individually or as part of a small prayer or larger church group, to take that time out, just for a few hours, a day or longer and 'Be still, and know that I am God' (Psalm 46:10 NIV), making time to witness that 'loveliness'.

If you would like more information about what happens on retreat, or for more information about the House of Retreat and the different facilities we can offer, please contact us:

www.retreathousepleshey.com
01245 237251
retreathouse@chelmsford.anglican.org

# Using *Quiet Spaces* with a group

*Sally Smith*

Advent is often a time when people are looking for some silence and some time away from the busyness and bustle of activity that typifies the lead-up to Christmas for many people. There is a desire to spend some time reflecting and noticing what is important about this season and creating the space in which to be touched by Jesus. Many people are looking for someone to lead their house group or other group in a reflection or meditation, and those of us known for praying in this way often find ourselves being called on to 'do something quiet' for a session. Below are some ways in which you might take some of the ideas presented in *Quiet Spaces* and use them with a group, possibly taking a couple of these suggestions to make an evening's or afternoon's session, or longer.

To bring all the ideas together, I suggest you set the scene by creating a crib or manger. You may have one you can use or borrow. Set it up without the baby, but do add some straw if you have it and some sheep and other stable animals if they are available. If you don't have access to a manger, you could make one by scrunching a small sheet or blanket into a round shape, with a hollow in the centre showing the space that is waiting for the baby to come and occupy it, waiting for the coming king, for Jesus. Again, add some animals if you have them, but don't worry if you don't. This will form a central visual focus for the group, as well as providing a place to symbolically place some of the things you will each have worked on during the session and so be able to offer them to God, to the coming Emmanuel, the king who will, and does, dwell with us.

Choose from the activities below, using the sections you feel drawn to or the ones you think your group will respond to best. You might like to use a couple of them over an evening or afternoon, but make sure they have two different approaches so people with different ways of praying will all find a way of engaging and drawing closer to God. The final activity will bring together all you have done separately and together in your time of prayer.

You may want to start by praying, asking God to be with each of you as you spend time with him, offering him the time to meet with each of you as he wills and asking that you might each allow the spirit to move in you and touch you as you need.

You could play the carol, 'O come, O come, Emmanuel' (available on YouTube) as you start. Sit around the empty manger waiting and anticipating the coming Emmanuel. Pause, don't be in a rush to move on, but allow time to wait together. You might suggest that people notice their emotions as they wait. What is it like looking at an empty crib? What is it like to wait? It may help some to have the words available for them to read as they are sung, or to use in the quiet after the singing has stopped.

# Stories of hope

The coming Emmanuel is a story of the coming of hope in a world that to many can seem bereft of hope. Have available some newspapers from the past week or two. Invite those present to look through the papers and to tear out any stories which are crying out for hope, stories of people who have, or could easily have, given up on hope. Suggest that they sit with the stories before the anticipated coming of the incarnate Christ, holding together the coming hope and the need for hope, allowing each to talk to the other. The stories could then be put into the manger as a way of offering them to God for the coming Christ to give them hope.

# Names of Christ

As we anticipate the birth of a baby there will be speculation on the names they will be given. Parents may discuss and argue over their favourites and what different names mean to them. Read Isaiah 9:6 and have copies of the words of 'O come, O come, Emmanuel' available. Invite each person to take one of the names for Jesus from the passage, the carol, or another name they know of, and to write it on a piece of card or paper. As they hold this name before God and anticipate the birth of that child they can write or draw around the name, illustrating and expanding on the meaning of the name for them and the God who is behind the name. Encourage them to listen to the God whose name they see before them and to receive what he wants to give them along with the gift of the one who bears the name. As the cards are added to the manger, the names could be read out loud.

# House of David

Joseph, and therefore Jesus, was from the house of David, the smallest of the tribes of Israel, and from Nazareth, noted for the words of Nathanael in John 1:46, 'Can anything good come from Nazareth?' Where locally might be your 'Nazareth'? A place where you wonder if anything good can come from that place. Don't name It, but invite people to consider where it might be and to notice their internal response as you suggest that Jesus could have come from there. Have some small objects (stones, buttons, dried beans, nails, etc.) available to represent the small places, people and tribes. Invite everyone to take one and, as they look and hold it, to imagine Christ coming from that place, and to imagine God in that insignificant, vulnerable item. Leave time to stay with the Christ who came to the small and ignored and vulnerable before inviting people to place the objects inside the manger, to be placed where God himself is to rest so the insignificant and vulnerable are received by and held close to Christ on earth.

Some may imagine themselves as that small, insignificant, good-for-nothing item. Invite them to dare to metaphorically place themselves in that intimate place with him, ready to receive from Christ.

## The Word became flesh

Slowly read John 1:1–5 and v. 14.

Invite those present to take one word or phrase from the passage and to hold on to it, to repeat it slowly to themselves and to allow it to become part of them. They should try to avoid analysing the passage, but instead try to allow the words and the Word to speak directly to them and to dwell in them. You may find it helps to read the passage three or four times, slowly. Leave a time of silence for each to work with their words and to allow it to become part of them.

## Annunciation

Lead the group as they imagine the scene and the actions from the annunciation (Luke 1:26–38). Spend time inviting them to imagine the scene, to see and smell and listen and feel what is around them; to watch Mary as she goes about her daily chores; then to watch as the angel appears and notice how they feel as well as how Mary reacts. Read aloud the words of Mary and of Gabriel.

Before the angel leaves Mary, he turns to each person present and they are invited to hear the message God has for them for now. Leave plenty of quiet before bringing the group back together.

End the session by placing a doll, or something to represent a baby (a jumper wrapped in a plain cloth or blanket will work), in the manger with the objects you have placed there. Allow time for individuals to connect Emmanuel, God with us, with the journey they have been on in the session.

You could end by playing 'O come, O come, Emmanuel' again and giving an opportunity for people to share something of that journey together. Encourage each to hold what they hear and to receive it as a gift to be cherished and valued. Discourage discussion, as this is about where people have been with God and about learning from each other.

# BRF Quiet Days

BRF Quiet Days are an ideal way of redressing the balance in our busy lives. Held in peaceful locations around the country, each one is led by an experienced speaker and gives the opportunity to reflect, be silent and pray, and, through it all, to draw closer to God.

Here is the programme for the final months of 2017:

**Thursday 21 September:** 'Living Deeply and Well in Later Life' led by Debbie Thrower at Old Alresford Place, Alresford, Hampshire SO24 9DH

**Thursday 9 November:** 'Marks upon the Heart: Pilgrim journeys, lessons for life' led by Sally Welch at The Carmelite Priory, Boars Hill, Oxford OX1 5HB

**Friday 10 November:** 'Hope in Unexpected Places' led by Ellie Hart at Shallowford House, Shallowford, Stone, Staffordshire ST15 0NZ

For further details and to book, please go to **brfonline.org.uk/events-and-quiet-days** or contact us at BRF, 15 The Chambers, Vineyard, Abingdon OX14 3FE; tel: +44 (0)1865 319700.

In *Pilgrim Journeys*, experienced pilgrim and writer Sally Welch explores the less-travelled pilgrim routes of the UK and beyond, through the eyes of the pilgrims who walk them. Each chapter explores a different aspect of pilgrimage, offering reflections and indicating some of the spiritual lessons to be learned that may be practised at home.

**Pilgrim Journeys**
*Pilgrimage for walkers and armchair travellers*
Sally Welch
ISBN 978 0 85746 513 9   £8.99

brfonline.org.uk

Finding God in all things, hearing God's voice for ourselves and others… the *Quiet Spaces Prayer Journal* will help you to develop and maintain a life of creative prayer. With space to write and quotations drawn from Christian tradition and from *Quiet Spaces* to aid reflection, this is ideal for you or as a gift for anyone wanting to deepen their prayer life.

**Quiet Spaces Prayer Journal**
ISBN 978 0 85746 524 5  £9.99

brfonline.org.uk

## QUIET SPACES SUBSCRIPTION FORM

All our Bible reading notes can be ordered online by visiting
**biblereadingnotes.org.uk/subscriptions**

If you and a minimum of **four** friends subscribe to *Quiet Spaces* or BRF's other Bible reading notes (*New Daylight*, *Day by Day with God*, *Guidelines*, *The Upper Room*), you can form a group. What's so good about being in a group? You pay the price of the notes only—postage is free for delivery to a UK address. (All notes are sent to one address.) All group orders are invoiced. No advance payment is required. For more information, visit **biblereadingnotes.org.uk/group-subscriptions** or contact the BRF office.

Title ............. First name/initials ............... Surname ..........................................

Address ...........................................................................................................

................................................................... Postcode .....................

Telephone ........................... Email ...................................................

---

**INDIVIDUAL SUBSCRIPTION** Please send *Quiet Spaces* beginning with the January 2018 / May 2018 / September 2018 issue (*delete as appropriate*):

|  | Quantity | UK | Europe | Rest of world |
|---|---|---|---|---|
| (per 3 issues) | ☐ | ☐ £16.50 | ☐ £24.60 | ☐ £28.50 |

Total enclosed £ ........................ (cheques should be made payable to 'BRF')

Please charge my MasterCard / Visa ☐ Debit card ☐ with £ ...................

Card no. ☐☐☐☐ ☐☐☐☐ ☐☐☐☐ ☐☐☐☐

Valid from ☐☐ ☐☐ Expires ☐☐ ☐☐ Security code* ☐☐☐

Last 3 digits on the reverse of the card

Signature* ............................................................ Date ....... / ....... / .......

*ESSENTIAL IN ORDER TO PROCESS YOUR ORDER

To set up a Direct Debit, please also complete the Direct Debit instruction on the reverse of this form.

---

**GROUP SUBSCRIPTION (UK only)** Please send *Quiet Spaces* beginning with the January 2018 / May 2018 / September 2018 issue (*delete as appropriate*):

Quantity ☐ (Current price per issue: £4.40)

Please invoice me: per issue / annually (*delete as appropriate*).

---

**Please return this form to:**
BRF, 15 The Chambers, Vineyard, Abingdon OX14 3FE

To read our terms and find out about cancelling your order, please visit **brfonline.org.uk/terms**.

The Bible Reading Fellowship is a Registered Charity (233280)

QS0317

## The Bible Reading Fellowship

# Instruction to your bank or building society to pay by Direct Debit

Please fill in the whole form using a ballpoint pen and return it to:
BRF, 15 The Chambers, Vineyard, Abingdon OX14 3FE

Service User Number: | 5 | 5 | 8 | 2 | 2 | 9 |

Name and full postal address of your bank or building society

| To: The Manager | Bank/Building Society |
|---|---|
| Address | |
| | |
| | |
| | Postcode |

Name(s) of account holder(s)

Branch sort code

Bank/Building Society account number

Reference number

**Instruction to your Bank/Building Society**
Please pay The Bible Reading Fellowship Direct Debits from the account detailed in this instruction, subject to the safeguards assured by the Direct Debit Guarantee. I understand that this instruction may remain with The Bible Reading Fellowship and, if so, details will be passed electronically to my bank/building society.

Signature(s)

Banks and Building Societies may not accept Direct Debit instructions for some types of account.

## DIRECT DEBIT PAYMENT

You can pay for your annual subscription to our Bible reading notes using Direct Debit. You need only give your bank details once, and the payment is made automatically every year until you cancel it. If you would like to pay by Direct Debit, please use the form opposite, entering your BRF account number under 'Reference number'.

You are fully covered by the Direct Debit Guarantee:

### The Direct Debit Guarantee

- This Guarantee is offered by all banks and building societies that accept instructions to pay Direct Debits.

- If there are any changes to the amount, date or frequency of your Direct Debit, The Bible Reading Fellowship will notify you 10 working days in advance of your account being debited or as otherwise agreed. If you request The Bible Reading Fellowship to collect a payment, confirmation of the amount and date will be given to you at the time of the request.

- If an error is made in the payment of your Direct Debit, by The Bible Reading Fellowship or your bank or building society, you are entitled to a full and immediate refund of the amount paid from your bank or building society.

- If you receive a refund you are not entitled to, you must pay it back when The Bible Reading Fellowship asks you to.

- You can cancel a Direct Debit at any time by simply contacting your bank or building society. Written confirmation may be required. Please also notify us.

This page is left blank for your notes.